HEAVEN

Gordon J. Keddie

ET Perspectives No. 2

Published by
EVANGELICAL TIMES
Faverdale North, Darlington, DL3 0PH, England

E-mail: theeditors@evangelicaltimes.org

Web: http://www.evangelicaltimes.org

First published 2006

British Library Cataloguing in Publication Data available

ISBN 0-9500129-2-0

Scripture quotations in this publication are from the Holy Bible, New King James Version, copyright © Thomas Nelson Inc, 1982. Used by permission. All rights reserved.

Printed in Great Britain
by Athenaeum Press, Gateshead, UK

HEAVEN

CONTENTS

page

Publisher's Note

The chapters of this booklet first appeared as a series of articles in *Evangelical Times*. In response to requests, these articles now appear in collected form — as the second of a series of booklets under the generic title *ET Perspectives*.

From time to time, *Evangelical Times*, a monthly newspaper, publishes series of articles on a variety of subjects, ranging from historical to theological, from practical Christian living to Bible exposition. The Editors feel that these series are often of sufficient interest to warrant being made available in their own right, and have therefore launched *ET Perspectives* as a means to this end. Each such series is normally of a length that lends itself to reprinting as a booklet — hence the present publication.

Our prayerful hope is that these inexpensive booklets will be of use in furthering the gospel of the glory of our Lord Jesus Christ and bringing men and women to a deeper knowledge of his unsearchable riches.

The Editors
Evangelical Times

Author's Preface

Most people like to believe there is a heaven — and that they will go there when they die. An ABC News poll in December 2005 found that 89% of all Americans believe in heaven and 75% expect to make it there. However, only 21% think you need to be a Christian (these are probably the Evangelicals) and just 22% of all who believe in heaven think we will have a body when we get there (that is, not all Evangelicals are clear on the resurrection of the body).

There has long been confusion (and presumption) on this topic. All religions have their versions of heaven and how to get there. Our multicultural interfaith world expects us to be accepting of everybody's views and not to press the exclusive claims of the only authoritative source on the subject that exists — the Bible.

But for every single person the day is coming when the truth will be revealed — when presumptuous certainties and vapid uncertainties will alike be tested and found wanting. God's Word is quite clear that there is salvation in no name under heaven save that of Jesus Christ (Acts 4:12). It also tells us a fair bit about heaven and a great deal about how to get there. 'God so loved the world that he gave his only begotten Son, that whoever believes in him should not perish but have everlasting life' (John 3:16). This little book seeks to point the way.

Gordon J. Keddie
Indianapolis, USA
January 2006

If then you were raised with Christ,
seek those things which are above,
where Christ is,
sitting at the right hand of God.
Set your mind on things above,
not on things on the earth.
For you died, and your life is hidden
with Christ in God.
When Christ who is our life appears,
then you also will appear with Him in glory.

(Colossians 3:1-4)

1. THINKING ABOUT HEAVEN

Do you think much about heaven? The Bible is full of eternity and constantly points us to the last judgement and the great divide between heaven and hell.

God has 'put eternity' in our hearts (Ecclesiastes 3:11) and he calls us to think seriously about where we will spend it. He sent his only-begotten Son to save his people from their sins and bring to heaven 'a great multitude which no one could number of all tribes, peoples and tongues' (Revelation 7:9).

Plan A or plan B?

Scripture refers to 'heaven' some 600 times. The New Testament is replete with references to the hope of heaven and the goal of glory, through saving faith in Jesus Christ. Yet heaven is given little thought, even by Christians. We often treat it like social security — something that will be there when we need it. In theory it is our goal, but in practice it is God's 'Plan B' for our lives. Meanwhile we stick with 'Plan A' (enjoying this life) for as long as possible.

Some, of course, reject the hope of heaven as so much 'pie-in-the-sky-by-and-by'. A. E. Housman's poem 'Ho Everyone that Thirsteth', takes its title from Isaiah 55:1 and alludes to John 7:37 and Ecclesiastes 12:5 but wearily proceeds to dismiss the teaching of the Scriptures as essentially unbelieveable and undesirable. He writes:

> *Ho everyone that thirsteth*
> *And hath the price to give,*
> *Come to the stolen waters,*
> *Drink and your soul shall live*

Come to the stolen waters
And leap the guarded pale,
And pull the flower in season
Before desire shall fail

It shall not last forever,
No more than earth or skies;
The lad that hopes for heaven
Shall live before he dies.

June suns, you cannot store them
To warm the winter's cold,
The lad that hopes for heaven
Shall fill his mouth with mould. [1]

In other words, there is no heaven — only six feet of earth when we die. So get sinning while you have time! Contrast this with Paul's words to the Colossians: 'If then you were raised with Christ, seek those things which are above, where Christ is, sitting at the right hand of God. Set your mind on things above, not on things on the earth' (Colossians 3:1-2). Clearly, God means us to think seriously and often about heaven and heaven's Lord.

Common excuses

Most people think there is a heaven and that they are going there. Yet few reflect on the subject beyond these bare assumptions. Why such neglect? Here are some of the most common excuses – even from some who regard themselves as Christians:

1. They complain, 'Heaven is weird and other-worldly'.

They buy into the idea that you can be 'so heavenly-minded that you're no earthly use'. Heaven is just not very practical. Never mind that Scripture teaches the very opposite!

2. 'Heaven is boring'. We accept the cartoon caricature — folks in white robes with halos, sitting on clouds and playing harps for ever: even more tedious, some might say, than going to church for a million years!

3. 'Heaven is too hard to think about'. Where is it? How does it work? What do you do? How do you get there? Yes, Jesus went up to heaven but it is hard to understand how. Besides, we have too much to do right here and now. Let's think about it later!

The real problem

The real problem, of course, is none of the above. It is that we are too tied to this life. The rich man in Jesus' story in Luke 12:16-21 is a classic case (more on this later; see chapter 9). He was too busy getting rich to think of either heaven or hell or even God himself. It is only too easy to 'walk by sight' when we should 'walk by faith' (2 Corinthians 5:7). We are alive, we are healthy and we have a life to live. In spite of all its problems, this world is a great place and what it offers really appeals to us.

Death and eternity seem far away — that is, until the day comes (as it will) when, like the rich fool, we will hear God say: 'This night your soul will be required of you' (Luke 12:20). If even Christians think this way, how much more the unconverted? To them the claims of Jesus are offensive and the prospects of facing a righteous Judge are just too awful to contemplate. It is small wonder that, like the rich fool in Jesus' parable, millions just put up the shutters of their hearts and minds. We blot out the light of God's Word precisely because it calls us to think on these things. Happy the way we are, we do the 'Felix thing' and put it off for a more 'convenient time' — the tomorrow that never comes (Acts 24:25).

Life is brief

Yet thinking about heaven really makes sense, and the reasons are pretty obvious. Let me ask two questions. Are you going to live here for ever? You know the answer to that one! So, where will you spend eternity? What are you really banking on? Be honest! When people flocked to John the Baptist, he got to the point right away, asking: 'Who warned you to flee the wrath to come?' (Luke 3:7). He then emphasised repentance and the fruits of a holy life. He charged them not to deceive themselves that they were right with God just because they went through certain religious motions. Here, then, is the 'bottom line': being born makes you fit for hell, but only being 'born again' can make you fit for heaven (John 3:3). There is only one name 'under heaven given among men by which we must be saved'. And that name is Jesus Christ (Acts 4:12). And you have only so long to deal with the matter, for the simple reason that 'it is appointed for men to die once, but after this the judgment' (Hebrews 9:27).

False hope

The easiest thing in the world is to trust in a false hope: to assume, as most people do, that God is too nice to put decent folks like us in hell. Scan the horizon of our culture and you find that belief in universal salvation is the norm. Dead celebrities (if we are to believe the tearful testimonies of their friends) are watching us benignly from heaven, however unbelieving or immoral their past lives. If singing *The Lord's my Shepherd* at funerals conveyed grace to dead sinners, no one would ever be lost! It begs the question people don't want to ask about the departed one: 'Was the Lord Jesus Christ his Shepherd?' Do the comforts of Psalm 23 apply to all and sundry — whatever they believe and however they live their lives? The answer of God's Word is too painfully obvious. But people will cling to false hopes rather than cling to Christ himself.

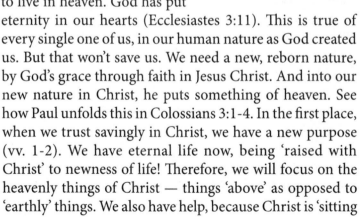

Live and grow

Are you already a Christian? Then understand that you will never be more fit to live on earth, than when you are fit to live in heaven. God has put eternity in our hearts (Ecclesiastes 3:11). This is true of every single one of us, in our human nature as God created us. But that won't save us. We need a new, reborn nature, by God's grace through faith in Jesus Christ. And into our new nature in Christ, he puts something of heaven. See how Paul unfolds this in Colossians 3:1-4. In the first place, when we trust savingly in Christ, we have a new purpose (vv. 1-2). We have eternal life now, being 'raised with Christ' to newness of life! Therefore, we will focus on the heavenly things of Christ — things 'above' as opposed to 'earthly' things. We also have help, because Christ is 'sitting at the right hand of God'. He is the King who reigns over all things in the interests of his people (Ephesians 1:20-22). All this adds up to a heaven-orientated mind-set in those who are truly united to Christ by faith. They 'think' heaven, 'think' Jesus, 'think God', and 'think' eternity into the time in which they live.

Priorities and promises

Secondly, therefore, Christians have new priorities. 'For you died and your life is hidden with Christ in God' (v. 3). Sin as a ruling enslavement has been put to death. The 'old man' died and earthbound priorities died with him. Your new life is with Christ in God. You are a new creation, with a new source of life, a new direction, new motives, new desires, and a new vision for time and eternity. Thirdly, we also have a new promise. Christ is our life. So when he appears at the end of history, we also 'will appear with him in glory' (v.4). What a prospect! This is not heaven as Plan B! No, this is God's glory revealed and Christ exalted as a Prince and a Saviour. This is reality, the real goal and eternal destination of the redeemed. This is heaven as Plan A — the true and ultimate home of the Lord's believing people, in heart, soul and mind. This heaven, even today, is the basis of my world-view and my eternal joy.

The future in the present

God wants us to live out this wonderful future in the present. Having our ultimate home in heaven is exactly what makes this world — God's world — also truly our home. Paul speaks of the awesome mystery of heaven in

1 Corinthians 2:9-10, quoting Isaiah 64:4 and 65:17: 'Eye has not seen, nor ear heard, nor have entered into the heart of man the things which God has prepared for those who love him'. But he does not stop with this statement of relative ignorance. He continues: 'But God has revealed them to us through his Spirit. For the Spirit searches all things, yes, the deep things of God'. Alive in Christ, and walking in the Spirit, we are called and equipped to be so heavenly-minded that we will be of great earthly use. We need to know more of heaven, more of glory, more of Christ. Let us then seek — and set our minds on — things above, where Christ is. Then we will live and labour in Christ's kingdom here, as those whose home is heaven.

NOTES

[1] Quoted in F. Kermode (ed.) *The Oxford Anthology of English Literature Vol. II* (Oxford University Press, 1973) p.2035

In this manner, therefore, pray:
Our Father in heaven,
Hallowed be your name.
your kingdom come.
Your will be done
on earth as it is in heaven.
Give us this day our daily bread.
And forgive us our debts,
As we forgive our debtors.
And do not lead us into temptation,
But deliver us from the evil one.
For yours is the kingdom
and the power and the glory forever.
Amen.

(Matthew 6:9-13;
see also Revelation 7:9-17)

2. OUR FATHER IS IN HEAVEN

In his letter to the Colossians, the apostle Paul challenges us to set our minds 'on things above, not things on the earth' (Colossians 3:1-4). The great motive for being truly heavenly-minded is that the believer is 'raised with Christ'. He has a new and everlasting life through faith in Jesus as his Saviour. Paul also reminds us that the risen Christ is even now in heaven, 'sitting at the right hand of God'. He is located there with our humanity, exalted as Lord and 'head over all things to the church' (Ephesians 1:22).

The Father

In thinking about Jesus' heavenly glory, we can easily forget the fact that God the Father is also there. Jesus is, after all, at the right hand of the Father. Indeed, it is the presence of the Father that defines Jesus' glory (John 17:5). You see this in Psalm 16:11 where David, in the language of prophecy, records Christ saying to the Father: 'In your presence is fullness of joy: at your right hand are pleasures forevermore'. The Father is the definition of glory, the source of joy forever and ever. The same thing is found in the Lord's Prayer, which begins: 'Our Father in heaven ...' (Matthew 6:9). I dare say that when we pray these words, we are so focused on the person of the Father, as the one who hears prayer (Psalm 65:1-2), that we hardly think of *where* he is. Our Father is 'in heaven'. He is not portrayed as being else-where or everywhere. It is from somewhere called heaven that his omnipresence reaches out into every corner of his creation.

Heaven is a real place

When I was a boy attending a theologically liberal church, I was taught that heaven was a state of mind rather than a location. Any idea of a place with real resurrection bodies, walking on real ground, in a new earth under new heavens, was dismissed as fanciful. Even a sound writer like Louis Berkhof says very little about heaven in his Systematic Theology but he is on target in saying that Scripture 'clearly presents heaven as a place'.[1] In fact, the Bible speaks of three distinct 'heavens'.

The first heaven is the sky above our heads, the atmosphere in which we live and breathe. In the Flood, we are told, 'the windows of heaven were opened' (Genesis 7:11). The psalmist says God 'covers the heavens with clouds' (Psalm 147:8), while Daniel speaks of 'the dew of heaven' (Daniel 4:5). The second heaven ('the heavens') is that of space and the heavenly bodies — the sun, moon and stars — the universe beyond the atmosphere. But the third heaven is where God dwells; it lies beyond our senses. It is explicitly called the 'third heaven' in 2 Corinthians 12:2, where Paul describes being 'caught up' in a unique experience of God's favour. Solomon prays repeatedly that the Lord would 'hear in heaven your dwelling place' (1 Kings 8:30,39,43,49), while Isaiah identifies God as 'the High and Lofty One who inhabits eternity' (Isaiah 57:15). In the Sermon on the Mount, Jesus exhorts: 'Let your light so shine before men, that they may see your good works and glorify your Father in heaven' (Matthew 5:16). There are many similar references in the New Testament, which also makes mention of 'the kingdom of heaven', 'bread from heaven' and the emphatic expression 'heaven itself', which is also 'God's throne' (Matthew 5:34; 12:50; 16:17; 18:10; Hebrews 9:24). The third heaven is therefore a location, although it clearly exists on an altogether different plane from the heavens above us.

Heaven is for Christians

Scripture assures us that Christians 'have a building from God, a house not made with hands, eternal in the heavens' (2 Corinthians 5:1). This contrasts with 'our earthly house, this tent', our mortal body which is 'destroyed' by death. Paul's point is that we will have bodies in heaven — resurrection bodies. Heaven must therefore be a created place where saved sinners and unfallen angels will live in the presence of the glorious God and the exalted Christ. Yet the immensity of God means that 'heaven and the heaven of heavens cannot contain [him]' (1 Kings 8:27). What a marvellous condescension to finite human beings it is, then, that the infinite God should manifest his glory in a place designed and adapted for everlasting human habitation — 'a new heavens and a new earth' (Isaiah 65:17; 66:22). The earth and the first two heavens will be reconstituted in what is now the third heaven, that the new humanity in Christ may be gloriously consummated in a new creation where 'righteousness dwells' (2 Peter 3:13).

Heaven is where Jesus reigns

Heaven is where Christians will be forever because the Lord Jesus Christ is there with his Father. First of all, Jesus is exalted in heaven to rule as sovereign over this world in the interests of his people. The Father's acceptance of Jesus' perfect sacrifice for sin guarantees his acceptance of those for whom Christ died and secures their salvation in time and eternity (Philippians 2:9-11; Ephesians 1:20-23; Hebrews 1:1-3; 1 Peter 3:22). Secondly, Jesus is preparing a place in heaven for believers, that they may be with him forever and behold his glory (John 14:2; 17:24; 2 Timothy 2:19). Thirdly, he is nurturing in believers a living hope that focuses on the anticipation of their heavenly inheritance (1 Peter 1:3-5). Fourthly, Jesus will come again to gather his people with him in the glory of heaven (John 14:3).

Jesus Christ, then, is the key that opens heaven for those who are saved by his grace. Indeed, it is only in and through his death as the only Mediator between God and man (1 Timothy 2:5), that sinners are adopted as sons to God, and so come to know him as their heavenly Father (John 14:6; Romans 8:15; Galatians 4:6). There is no heaven and no Father-God for anyone apart from saving faith in Jesus Christ.

Heaven on earth

This has tremendous practical implications for the way we live day by day. With every passing day, 'our salvation is nearer than when we first believed' (Romans 13:11). Setting 'our minds on things above' should be second nature for those who love the Lord. Our praying is to begin with 'Our Father in heaven', because our new life in Christ has its source and its goal in heaven.

In one of his parables, Christ tells us: 'Then the King will say to those on his right hand, "Come, you blessed of My Father, inherit the kingdom prepared for you from the foundation of the world"' (Matthew 25:34). We are therefore called to live our lives on earth *sub specie aeternitatis* — that is, with reference to eternity and in the sight of our Father in heaven. We are called to practise heavenly holiness: 'Therefore you shall be perfect, just as your Father in heaven is perfect' (Matthew 5:43-48). Glory calls us to godliness, striving to live as those who are laying up treasure in heaven: 'For where your treasure is, there will

your heart be also'(Matthew 6:19-23).
Where is your heart? Is it set on heaven
or rooted in this world?

We are promised that as we follow
the Lord, he will guide us in life and
bring us to heaven. Paul tells Timothy how to persevere in a faithful life,
especially when buffeted by sufferings
for the faith. He says: 'For this reason I
also suffer these things; nevertheless I

am not ashamed, for I know whom I have believed and am
persuaded that he is able to keep what I have committed
to him until that Day' (2 Timothy 1:12). He does not cling
to some hope of earthly relief or success, but anchors his
confidence in the Day of Christ's return and his consummation of the gospel of the kingdom. Heaven is the great
goal, not some earthly glory.

In Psalm 73:23-24, Asaph agonises over the challenge
of living for God in an evil world, where the wicked seem to
enjoy successful lives and easy deaths. He found the answer,
of course, in terms of eternity — of sin, judgement and
salvation. Accordingly, he praises the Lord as his Father in
heaven and looks forward to the glory yet to be revealed:

> *Yet evermore I am with thee:*
> *Thou holdest me by my right hand.*
> *And thou, ev'n thou, my guide shalt be;*
> *Thy counsel shall my way command;*
> *And afterward in glory bright*
> *Shalt thou receive me to thy sight.*

NOTES

[1] L. Berkhof, *Systematic Theology* (Banner of Truth, 1957) p.737 [Berkhof
devotes one page of 738 to the subject of heaven].

For we know that if our earthly house, this tent,
is destroyed, we have a building from God,
a house not made with hands, eternal in the heavens.
For in this we groan, earnestly desiring to be clothed with
our habitation which is from heaven,
if indeed, having been clothed, we shall not be found naked.
For we who are in this tent groan, being burdened,
not because we want to be unclothed, but further clothed,
that mortality may be swallowed up by life.

Now He who has prepared us for this very thing is God, who
also has given us the Spirit as a guarantee.
So we are always confident, knowing that while we are at
home in the body we are absent from the Lord.

For we walk by faith, not by sight.

We are confident, yes, well pleased rather to be absent from
the body and to be present with the Lord.
Therefore we make it our aim, whether present or absent,
to be well pleasing to Him.
For we must all appear before the judgement seat of Christ,
that each one may receive the things done in the body,
according to what he has done, whether good or bad.
Knowing, therefore, the terror of the Lord, we persuade
men; but we are well known to God,
and I also trust are well known in your consciences.

(2 Corinthians 5:1-11)

3. A BUILDING FROM GOD

One of the most searching challenges in the Bible is surely Solomon's charge to young people in Ecclesiastes 12. He first says: 'Remember your Creator in the days of your youth, before the difficult days come, and the years draw near when you say, I have no pleasure in them' (12:1). He then describes in relentless detail the progressive loss of faculties in old age — no less powerfully for the poetic language — until 'man goes to his eternal home, and the mourners go about the streets' (vv. 3-5). It is a simple and unanswerable argument. Our bodies are wearing out, our 'spirit' will soon return to God who gave it, and we urgently need to turn to God (vv. 7, 13-14). How we respond to this challenge will determine where we spend eternity and how we spend the rest of our lives.

Responding to realities

Sometimes people react with anger. Sometimes they respond by denying the obvious, trying hard not to think of death and eternity. They try to 'live life to the full' as if this life will never come to a reckoning, either in time or eternity. What a liberation it is, however, to accept both God's diagnosis and cure! To accept that our 'outward man' is perishing but that, through faith in Jesus Christ as Saviour, the 'inward man' is renewed day by day, even in the face of physical decline (2 Corinthians 4:16). But Paul does not leave the matter there. He looks beyond death and into eternity: 'For we know that if our earthly house, this tent, is destroyed, we have a building from God, a house not made with hands, eternal in the heavens' (2 Corinthians 5:1ff).

He then unfolds a three-part exposition of God's answer to the brevity of life.

A building from God

Firstly, there is a promise. 'This corruptible must put on incorruption, and this mortal must put on immortality', so that 'death is swallowed up in victory' (1 Corinthians 15:53-55). Paul employs a double contrast. Our 'earthly house ... this tent' (our present body) will be replaced by a 'building from God' (our resurrection body). The former will be 'destroyed' but the latter remains 'eternal in the heavens'. How does faith respond to these things? By earnestly desiring our new body from heaven (vv. 2-3). We want to be 'clothed', not 'naked' — to be whole people in heaven, body and soul. Paul knows we will not be 'clothed' until the resurrection day, when Christ returns, but that makes his anticipation all the more enthusiastic.

Desire

Notice also that this desire reflects not just his consolation but his aim, goal and hope! It is something better than the best we have in this present age. If you are not longing for heaven, you are still too attached to the earth. The reason for earnestly desiring a new body is that in this life we 'groan, being burdened' (v. 4). Our present existence has inherent problems that trouble us profoundly.

Edward Donnelly observes: 'At present, our bodies hinder us in our Christian living'. They 'hunger, lust and grow tired. Their demands can distract and divert us from God'.[1] So many Christians, even, don't want to hear this kind of thing. Why? Because they underestimate their own corruption and they underestimate the glory of heaven. Heaven, however, is a lot more that just being alive in our present bodies, minus illnesses and physical defects. Things will be different in heaven, for 'the Lord Jesus Christ ... will transform our lowly body [to] be conformed to his glorious body' (Philippians 3:21). We shall be changed and 'further clothed, that mortality may be swallowed up by life' (v. 4).

Clothed

In a passage of striking brilliance, A. A. Hodge likens this transformation to the instantaneous restoration of sight and hearing to one born blind and deaf: 'Some such experience will be yours and mine when we are clothed upon with our glorified bodies on the morning of the resurrection. Coming up from rural and urban graveyards, rising before the awful whiteness of the throne and the intolerable glory of him that sits thereon, and passing through the interminable ranks of flaming seraphs and diademed archangels, the perfect senses of our new bodies will bring us at once into the presence of the whole universe, of the music of all its spheres, and of the effulgence of all its suns — of the most secret working of all its forces, and of the recorded history of all its past'.[2]

Neither does Paul follow Plato's idea of the body as a

tomb from which the soul awaits liberation. He does not want to be rid of his body because matter itself is evil. Nor is Paul a materialist, clinging to life and hoping for the day when all that ails us will be cured and life-expectancy extended indefinitely. No; the life of heaven is his goal and the focus of his deepest desire. And that life is qualitatively different — and the difference is glory from God.

Certainty from God

Secondly, God makes a pledge (vv. 5-8). How can we be confident about this heavenly body to come? Paul offers three answers, which reflect the relationship of the Triune God to his believing people.

1. God the Father is himself our certainty. He has 'prepared us for this very thing' (v. 5). This is an appeal to the truth of the Word of God — his self-revelation as the sovereign God who created us at the beginning and recreates us by the gospel of Christ.

2. The Holy Spirit is given as a guarantee (v. 5). This is an appeal to the work of God in the experience of believers, as the heavenly Comforter ministers in their hearts and lives (John 14:26; 15:26; 16:13).

3. The Lord Jesus Christ is the focus of our faith, hope and love. The exercise of faith confirms the hope of a new body from God in heaven (vv. 6-8). We are 'always confident', says Paul, and this for several reasons.

For one thing, being 'at home in this body' means we are 'absent from the Lord' (v. 6). The tatters appearing in our earthly tent, painful as they are, just indicate that we are drawing closer to our real home, where we shall be with our dear Saviour. Furthermore, we understand this because 'we walk by faith, not by sight' (v. 7). The Christian is more impressed by what he believes than by what he sees. He looks in the mirror and sees his days ebbing away. He looks to Christ by faith and sees everlasting glory. As he 'walks' by faith, his hope in God's promise is enlarged and his experience of God's grace deepened. Does this touch your experience today and every day? I rather fear that many Christians are afraid to leave this body, this life and this world to be with the Lord. But if we truly love Christ we will desire to be with him.

Living for God

Thirdly, there is a practical programme. Earnest longing for heaven is the engine that powers effective living on earth. It ne-gates the 'too heaven-ly minded, no earthly  use' idea, and the claim of secular culture that 'this world is all there is'. Many Christians unwittingly 'buy into' these worldly attitudes. They neither hope actively for heaven, nor relate to heaven as they live in the world. Paul there-fore delineates the heaven-focused discipleship that makes for practical Christian living. First comes commitment to pleasing God (v. 9). The starting point of godly behaviour is the consideration that one day we shall be present with the Lord. It follows that whether 'present or absent' we seek to be 'well pleasing to him'. Further motivation comes from the conviction that we are accountable to Christ. We must appear before his judgement seat to answer for our actions (v. 10). The Lord's people are already saved, and will be acquitted in that day. But that future judgement calls us to faithfulness in the details of living, informing our motives and actions as we submit even now to Christ's Lordship.

To live is Christ

Such solemn anticipations demand conscientiousness in our service to the Lord in a world that will perish under Christ's righteous judgement unless brought to salvation in him (v.11). This constrains Paul to proclaim the gospel faithfully and urgently (see Romans 1:16). He knows 'the terror of the Lord' because he understands the significance of coming judgement for the lost. Paul was not disobedient to 'the heavenly vision' of the Damascus Road. Throughout his ministry (Acts 26:19-20) he sought to 'persuade men'. And he can appeal to the witness of heaven ('we are well known to God') and the testimony of believers ('I also trust are well known in your consciences') that he has a good conscience before the Lord. The watchword for the Christian's life is beautifully stated in Philippians 1:21-24: 'For to me, to live is Christ, and to die is gain'.

Paul is happy to live in his tattered tent, but will be even happier when clothed with the heavenly building from God: 'What I shall choose I cannot tell. For I am hard-pressed between the two, having a desire to depart and be with Christ, which is far better. Nevertheless to remain in the flesh is more needful for you'. Let us embrace the promises of God, and live the heavenward life in Christ each day.

NOTES

[1] E. Donnelly, *Heaven and Hell* (Banner of Truth, 2002) p.108

[2] A. A. Hodge, *Evangelical Theology* (Banner of Truth, 1996) p.380

Now I saw a new heaven and a new earth,
for the first heaven and the first earth
had passed away. Also there was no more sea.
Then I, John, saw the holy city, New Jerusalem,
coming down out of heaven from God,
prepared as a bride adorned for her husband.
And I heard a loud voice from heaven saying,
"Behold, the tabernacle of God is with men,
and he will dwell with them,
and they shall be his people.
God himself will be with them and be their God. And
God will wipe away every tear from their eyes; there
shall be no more death, nor sorrow, nor crying. There
shall be no more pain,
for the former things have passed away..."

Then one of the seven angels who had the seven
bowls filled with the seven last plagues came to me and
talked with me, saying, "Come, I will show you the
bride, the Lamb's wife". And he carried me away in the
Spirit to a great and high mountain,
and showed me the great city, the holy Jerusalem,
descending out of heaven from God,
having the glory of God...

(Revelation 21:1-17)

4. THE GEOGRAPHY OF GLORY (1)

What is heaven like? In cartoons and TV ads it is depicted as a cold and ethereal place. If it has any 'land', it is a bit like the North Pole — all white under a bright sky. More often there is just sky with puffy clouds supporting people in white robes playing harps and cracking jokes. Such caricatures may be amusing, but they are a mockery of the Christian conception of heaven and life after death. For all the rash of books on 'near-death' experiences and 'day-trips to the next life', the only source of hard information on what heaven will be like is God's Word, the Bible. And of all the passages that address this subject, Revelation 21 is the most vivid and detailed. It reveals a rich landscape with magnificent buildings. It is populated by the innumerable multitude of God's elect, who live, work and worship around the awesome presence of God the Father, the Lord Jesus Christ and the host of heaven.

We will consider first what I will call 'the geography of glory'. This is unfolded in Revelation 2:1-21. The 'experience of glory', which will be the subject of the next chapter, is opened up in Revelation 21:22-22:5. The former concerns what heaven will 'look like' — how we are to think of it as an environment. The latter describes what it will mean to live in that new heaven and new earth as people of God, resurrected and transformed.

In this and the subsequent chapter, we shall consider three aspects of the eternal heaven to come: a reconstituted creation (21:1), a recreated city (21:2, 9-21), and a redeemed citizenry (21:3-8).

A reconstituted creation

Heaven, as presently constituted, is invisible to us. It is the dwelling of God the Father and his exalted Son, the crucified and risen Jesus. It is 'the third heaven' (2 Corinthians 12:2) from which 'the Lord looks down ... upon the children of men, to see if there are any that did understand, who seek God' (Psalm 14:2). This heaven, as Edward Donnelly has written, 'is the arena of glory'[1] and when Christ returns, it will embrace the new earth, so that heaven and earth are one visible whole. Glorious as it is already, heaven will undergo certain developments before the purposes of God in redemption are completed. Several components of the eternal heaven are presently missing. For example, the history of creation remains to be consummated. The 'kingdoms of this world' have yet to become 'the kingdoms of our Lord and of his Christ' (Revelation 11:15).

The full number of God's people — the population of heaven — has yet to be saved. Many millions, perhaps, are yet to be born before this final day (Psalm 22:31). Only at the end of history will God 'send His angels with a great sound of a trumpet, and they will gather together his elect from the four winds, from one end of heaven to the other' (Matthew 24:31).

Earth transformed

John sees that 'the first heaven and the first earth had passed away' (compare Matthew 5:18; 24:35; 2 Peter 3:10; 1 John 2:17). Psalm 102:26 says: 'They will perish, but you will endure; yes, they will all grow old like a garment; like a cloak you will change them, and they will be changed'. This transformation is summarised in a startling way by John's declaration that 'there was no more sea'. Hendriksen points out: 'At present the sea is the emblem of unrest and conflict. The roaring, raging, agitated, tempest-tossed waters, the waves perpet-

ually engaged in combat with one another s y m b o l i s e the nations of the world in their conflict and unrest'.[2] For example, Isaiah says 'the wicked are like the troubled sea, when it

cannot rest, whose waters cast up mire and dirt' (Isaiah 57:20). John Martin (1789-1854), a British artist well known for his apocalyptic canvases, painted 'The Plains of Heaven' to illustrate Revelation 21. It is in the Tate Gallery in London. A fleet of gondolas is bringing the redeemed to the shore of a great lake, to be met by angels in white robes. The holy city is supposedly descending in the clouds and the landscape is vast and beautiful, filled with flowers, the cedars of Lebanon, and the palm trees of Elim. There is no sun, but light suffuses everything. There is no more sea, but rivers and lakes abound. This is not your standard angels-with-harps-on-a-cloud cartoon, but one man's serious attempt to evoke something of the renewed world of the glory to come.

Consolidation

There will be a consolidated 'new heaven' and 'new earth'. This puts Revelation 21:1 in proper perspective. John sees a final transformation at the end of history in which heaven and earth are reconstituted as one entity which includes God's heaven. This is also prophesied elsewhere in Scripture (Isaiah 65:17-19; 66:22-23). We naturally think of going to heaven when we die and this is true enough. As the Shorter Catechism says[3]: 'The souls of believers are at their death made perfect in holiness (Hebrews 12:23) and do immediately pass into glory (2 Corinthians 5:1,6,8; Philippians 1:23; Luke 23:43)'. But our hope reaches even further — to the day of resurrection. In 2 Peter 3 the full scope of our heavenly hope is declared — that ultimate, eternal, final form of heaven in which all things are made new, including our resurrected bodies and a reconstituted world.

God has his own timetable. He is both reserving this present world for a fiery end, and bringing salvation to those in future generations who will not 'perish but ... come to repentance' (v. 9). Only when the latter is accomplished will the former take its course. Then 'the day of the Lord will come as a thief in the night, in which the heavens will pass away with a great noise, and the elements will melt with fervent heat: both the earth and the works that are in it will be burned up' (v.10).

Peter also makes practical applications. First, we ought to live godly lives (v.11). Second, we ought to be 'looking for and hastening the coming of the day of God' (v.12). And third, we should look expectantly for 'new heavens and a new earth in which righteousness dwells' (v.13). The creation itself will also be renewed. It will cease to groan under the burden imposed by human sin and be 'delivered from the bondage of corruption into the glorious liberty of the children of God' (Romans 8:20-22). Our present defiled environment will become the new environment in which God's people will live for ever. There will be no Chernobyls, no Love Canals, and no Exxon Valdez's in the 'new heaven and the new earth'.

A recreated city

John also sees a recreated city (21:2, 9-21), a 'new Jerusalem' descending from heaven from God. This 'holy city' is represented as already existing. It descends from heaven as it presently is, so as to become the centre-piece of the new earth. The expression 'holy city' reaches back to the 'Salem' of Melchizedek, who prefigured Christ (Hebrews 7:1-21). It relates to David's Jerusalem, where God presenced himself in the Temple, and to Mount Zion, which in Scripture represents the church as the people of God (Galatians 4:26-28; Hebrews 12:22). The centrality of Jerusalem to the Old Testament church is expressed in the lament of the exiled Jews in Babylon: 'If I forget you, O Jerusalem, let my right hand forget its skill! If I do not remember you, let my tongue cling to the roof of my mouth — if I do not exalt Jerusalem above my chief joy' (Psalm 137:5). 'Among the many illustrations that convey the nature of heaven to us', observes E. M. Bounds, 'the illustration of a city is the most striking ... A city teems with life in its richest and most strenuous form. It has never felt the chill of death ... Graves have never been dug there ... Heaven is a city of life ... Heaven knows no tears and has never felt a sorrow. It is filled with eternal, brilliant and vibrant life'.[4]

The church of Christ

This is what Abraham was looking for when 'he waited for the city which has foundations, whose builder and maker is God' (Hebrews 11:10). This is Jerusalem as the church: 'But you have come to Mount Zion and to the city of the living God, the heavenly Jerusalem, to an innumerable company of angels, to the general assembly and church of the first-born who are registered in heaven, to God the Judge of all, to the spirits of just men made perfect' (Hebrews 12:22-23). Jerusalem the place is not the point. The real meaning is in the words 'prepared as a bride adorned for her husband' (compare John 3:29; Revelation 22:17). The imagery is straight from the prophets as they refer to the relationship between God and his people (Isaiah 49:18; 62:5; Jeremiah 33:11). Christ is the bridegroom and the church is 'the bride, the Lamb's wife' (Revelation 21:9; Isaiah 61:10).

NOTES

[1] E. Donnelly, *Heaven and Hell* (Banner of Truth, 2002) p.74

[2] W. Hendrikson, *More than Conquerors* (Baker Book House Company, 1994) p.199

[3] *Westminster Shorter Catechism* (www.reformed.org/documents/WSC_frames.html) Q.37

[4] E. M. Bounds, *Catching a Glimpse of Heaven* (Whitaker House, 1985) pp. 29-30

Now the wall of the city had twelve foundations,
and on them were the names
of the twelve apostles of the Lamb.
And he who talked with me had a gold reed
to measure the city, its gates, and its wall.
The city is laid out as a square;
its length is as great as its breadth.
And he measured the city with the reed:
twelve thousand furlongs.
Its length, breadth, and height are equal.
Then he measured its wall:
one hundred and forty-four cubits, according
to the measure of a man, that is, of an angel.
The construction of its wall was of jasper;
and the city was pure gold, like clear glass.
The foundations of the wall of the city were adorned
with all kinds of precious stones ...
But I saw no temple in it, for the Lord God
Almighty and the Lamb are its temple.
The city had no need of the sun or of the moon to shine
in it, for the glory of God illuminated it.
The Lamb is its light.
And the nations of those who are saved shall walk
in its light, and the kings of the earth bring
their glory and honour into it.
Its gates shall not be shut at all by day
— there shall be no night there

(Revelation 21:14-25)

5. THE GEOGRAPHY OF GLORY (2)

In the previous chapter we began to consider what I called 'the geography of glory'. Continuing this theme we now come to verses 9-21 of Revelation 21, which picture heaven as a glorious city. These verses recapitulate and expand upon 21:2 in order to show us something of the glorious construction of the new Jerusalem. Bear in mind that this is a vision, not a video! The angel himself lays down the interpretative principle we are to apply to his description of the city: 'Come, I will show you the bride...' (21:9). This city is the church triumphant in heaven, and soon to be situated on the new earth. We are not being given a street-plan of heaven, but a symbolic evocation of the corporate life of the people of God. That is not to say that there will not be a visible city of God in space and (endless) time. The new earth will be three-dimensional, with a real city in a real creation with real people in real physical bodies living in real dwellings.

City of light, safety and majesty

This city has three leading features. They are as follows. Firstly, it is full of light (v.11). It is illuminated by the glory of God and Jesus is its lamp. The sun and the moon are not needed and there is no more night (v.23,25). This is more than physical illumination, although it is that. It is also the complete triumph of spiritual light — light as opposed to darkness — representing truth and righteousness over against the now-banished powers of evil. Secondly, it is safe and secure (vv. 12-14,25). There are massive walls, but they are not needed for defence. There are gates made each of a single pearl, guarded by angels (the 'pearly gates' of jokes and cartoons). The gates are never closed. We are not besieged. The whole new universe of glory will be ours, with neither danger nor hindrance. This tells us that the kingship of Christ will then be without challenge of any kind. Indeed, 'the kings of the earth bring their glory and honour into it' (v. 24; Revelation 11:15). He has delivered us 'from the evil one' for Christ's is 'the kingdom and the power and the glory for ever' (Matthew 6:13). There will be no warring nations, no squabbling families, no contradiction whatsoever of the will and pleasure of God and his redeemed.

Thirdly, the city is magnificent and imposing (vv. 15-21). It is constructed with precious stones and gold. The city is 1,500 miles square and covers an area of 2.25 million square miles — about equal to most of the USA east of the Mississippi. It would provide enough room, says John MacArthur, to house about 11 billion people![1] The point is not that we should estimate the number of the elect, but that there will be space enough in heaven for them all. 'In my Father's house', said Jesus, 'are many mansions' (John 14:2).

The city is also 1,500 miles high, which makes it a cube rising way up into space. Again, remember this is a vision, not an artist's impression or a photograph. The symbolism comes to life when you realise that the Holy of Holies in Solomon's Temple was also a cube, but only 30 feet each way (1 Kings 6:20). The New Jerusalem is the new Holy of Holies, the place where God dwells in covenant among his people. He and the Lamb are the final temple (v. 22), 'the tabernacle of God' that is for ever 'with men' (v. 3). This is 'man's chief end' come to fulfilment, namely, 'to glorify God, and to enjoy him for ever'.[2] Is this your goal for your life?

A city full of believing people

Who will inhabit heaven? The vision provides its own answer. The inhabitants will be those who are 'the bride' of Christ (v. 2). The fact that the gates of the city are named for the twelve tribes of Israel, and the foundations of the walls for the twelve apostles (vv. 12-14), indicates that a redeemed citizenry is in view, that is, those whose names 'are written in the Lamb's book of

life' (v. 27). This is confirmed by three distinct emphases in the passage, the last of which is a call to people of every era to repent of sin and believe in the Lord. Firstly, God comes to us for ever: 'God himself will be with them and be their God' (v. 3). The relationship between God and (the new) humanity is resolved completely and permanently by his unhindered presence and fellowship with them. They, for their part, are reconciled through 'the blood of the everlasting covenant' in Jesus Christ (Hebrews 13:20).

Secondly, God saves us from all evil, and salvation comes to its final victory: 'God will wipe away every tear ... [and] make all things new' (vv. 4-5). The condition of God's people will be resolved fully and permanently by the removal of all the effects of sin and its corruption. There will be no death, sorrow, crying or pain. Thirdly, God calls us to account even now (vv. 6-8). The application is that every one of us is accountable to the sovereign God right now. On which side of God's victory will you end up? As we might expect in a vision of the final consummation of God's plan for mankind, the destinies of believers and unbelievers are set out in relentless certitude and as accomplished fact: 'It is done! I am the Alpha and the Omega, the Beginning and the End'.

Nevertheless, the door is left open for anyone who will listen to God. In the first place, God promises new life to all who will come to him: 'I will give of the fountain of the water of life freely to him who thirsts' (v. 6). He is 'the fountain of living waters' (Jeremiah 2:13; 17:13), and that fountain is opened in Christ (Zechariah 13:1). Jesus declares that those who believe in him will never hunger or thirst (John 4:14; 6:35). He puts the responsibility where it belongs. Do you thirst for salvation from your sins and eternal life? Will you, like the jailer in Philippi, believe in the Lord Jesus Christ that you might be saved (Acts 16:31)?

Overcoming

In the second place, God promises each believer that he will 'inherit all things' as his adopted child and heir (v. 7). Christ is not ashamed to call those who believe in him his 'brothers' (Hebrews 2:11). The emphasis is that a believer is one who 'overcomes' (v. 7). This stresses that a living faith persists and presses toward the goal of the upward call of God in Christ Jesus (Philippians 3:14). The believing soul has 'the Spirit of adoption by whom we cry out, "Abba, Father"'. For 'The Spirit himself bears witness with our spirit that we are children of God, and if children, then heirs — heirs of God and joint heirs with Christ, if indeed we suffer with him, that we may also be glorified together' (Romans 8:15-17).

Eternal destiny

Finally, God reminds us of the default destination for those who will not repent (v. 8). The unrepentant and unbelieving will be 'turned into hell' (Psalm 9:17). This is the 'second death' — the unending state of spiritual deadness under God's righteous judgement. This is a sombre note on which to end a section on how all things are to be made new. The drama of the moment, however, has the clear intent of underlining the urgency of the issue for every living human being. The coming of Christ, and the revealing of the new heaven and new earth, may yet be long delayed in terms of human history. But the eternal destiny of those who are alive today will be settled in a very short time (anything from minutes to decades!) This is a blink of God's eye. If we have any sense at all, we must know that the moment of decision is upon us. We must close with Christ and embrace him as our Saviour. Peter urges us to make the proper application in our lives: 'Therefore, since all these will be dissolved, what manner of persons ought you to be in holy conduct and godliness, looking for and hastening the coming of the day of God, because of which the heavens will be dissolved, being on fire, and the elements will melt with fervent heat? Nevertheless we, according to his promise, look for new heavens and a new earth in which righteousness dwells' (2 Peter 3:11-13).

NOTES

[1] J. MacArthur, *The Glory of Heaven* (Crossway Books, 1998) pp. 107-108
[2] *Westminster Shorter Catechism* (www.reformed.org/documents/WSC_frames.html) Q.1

*But I saw no temple in it, for the Lord God Almighty
and the Lamb are its temple.
The city had no need of the sun or of the moon to
shine in it, for the glory of God illuminated it.
The Lamb is its light.
And the nations of those who are saved shall walk
in its light, and the kings of the earth
bring their glory and honour into it.
Its gates shall not be shut at all by day
(there shall be no night there).
And they shall bring the glory and the honour
of the nations into it.
But there shall by no means
enter it anything that defiles, or causes
an abomination or a lie,
but only those who are written
in the Lamb's Book of Life.
And he showed me a pure river of water of life,
clear as crystal, proceeding from the throne of God
and of the Lamb. In the middle of its street, and on
either side of the river, was the tree of life, which bore
twelve fruits, each tree yielding its fruit every month.
The leaves of the tree were for the healing
of the nations. And there shall be no more curse,
but the throne of God and of the Lamb shall be in it,
and His servants shall serve him. They shall see his
face, and his name shall be on their foreheads.
There shall be no night there: They need no lamp nor
light of the sun, for the Lord God gives them light.
And they shall reign forever and ever.*

(Revelation 21:22 - 22:5)

6. THE EXPERIENCE OF HEAVEN

What will heaven be like? We have already seen, in Revelation 21: 1-21, something of what we called 'the geography of glory' — what heaven will look like when this world is wound up at 'the end of the age' (Matthew 13:49; 24:3; 28:20). But now the focus changes to the experience of glory — what it will be like to live in that new heaven and new earth as the saved, sanctified and glorified people of God.

Vision

We must again remember that this is a vision and not a video. Jonathan Edwards comments: 'There is nothing upon earth that will suffice to represent to us the glory of heaven.'[1] The glimpses of glory that God gave in the past — for example, to Moses on Sinai and to the disciples at Jesus' transfiguration — all point to something far greater, namely, the glory of heaven. The visions of heaven and the holy city represent realities which will not only be seen and felt, but which will transcend all the foretastes given us in Scripture and the most spectacular sights we have seen in this present world. Heaven will be a feast for the senses and the soul, and excite our wonder for all eternity.

Our passage reveals something of what it means to be 'partakers of the inheritance of the saints in light' (Colossians 1:12). It unfolds six particular qualities of that experience.

Unhindered worship

Firstly, there will be unhindered worship. There is 'no temple' in heaven (21:22). This must have been astounding to both Jewish and Gentile Christians, who associated public worship with buildings dedicated to that purpose. Had not God visibly manifested his presence as the Shekinah — the Glory-cloud — in the tabernacle and the temple (Exodus 40:44-45; 1 Kings 8:11)? To have no dedicated location for worship seems to imply no worship at all! Without a temple, how shall we 'enter into his gates with thanksgiving, and into his courts with praise' (Psalm 100:4)?

The answer is that 'the Lord God Almighty and the Lamb are its temple'. The Jerusalem temple was destroyed in A.D. 70 ending animal sacrifices for ever. Even before that, they had been rendered obsolete by the sacrificial death of Jesus, 'the Lamb of God'. The tabernacle and temple, the priesthood and offerings, were only symbols of Christ and the gospel of salvation through his shed blood (Luke 22:20; cf. Exodus 22:2-3). It is therefore impossible for there to be a temple in heaven (nor should anyone attempt to rebuild the temple here on earth). Christ is the final temple, the great high priest, and the once-for-all sufficient sacrifice for sin.

The triune God is the ever-present centre of life in heaven. In a sense, 'the worship never stops'.[2] There is pure worship in the assembly of the just (Hebrews 12:23), but in heaven we will enjoy unhindered worship with a perfection that eludes us here. In glory, 'we shall always be with the Lord' (1 Thessalonians 4:17) and 'dwell in the house of the Lord all the days of [our] life, to behold the beauty of the Lord and to inquire in his temple' (Psalm 27:4; 23:6).

Ever-dawning light

Secondly, there will be ever-dawning light. There is 'no need of the sun' for light in heaven! (21:23) This too runs counter to all our experience. There 'the moon will be disgraced and the sun ashamed; for the Lord of Hosts will reign on Mount Zion ... gloriously' (Isaiah 24:23). Heaven will be flooded with ever-dawning light, for 'the glory of God illuminated it, and the Lamb is its light'. Uncreated light will manifest the glory of God's being and presence. We shall see God (Matthew 5:8), behold Jesus' glory (John 17:24) and 'be like him, for we shall see him as he is' (1 John 3:2). Light and vision are also used in Scripture,  figuratively, of spiritual insight and discernment. Paul says: 'God who commanded light to shine out of darkness ... has shone in our hearts to give the light of the knowledge of the glory of God in the face of Jesus Christ' (2 Corinthians 4:6). That 'the eyes of the blind shall be opened' (Isaiah 35:5) foresees not only the conversion of the lost, but the perfect vision, physical and spiritual, of the people of God in heaven.

Unclouded love

Thirdly, we shall experience unclouded love. It is no surprise that 'the nations of those who are saved shall walk in [heaven's] light' (21:24). The Greek for 'nations' is *ethne*, from which we get the English 'ethnic'. In this world, ethnicity often means discrimination, strife, oppression, and even extermination! There will still be 'ethnicity' in heaven, but all will share the same love. All one in Christ Jesus, they will love one another with the love with which Christ has loved them (Galatians 2:20,28; John 13:34; 15:12). The reason is 'the kings of the earth bring their glory and honour into it'; that is, they will acknowledge Christ as King of kings: 'The kingdoms of this world have become the kingdom of our Lord and of his Christ, and he shall reign for ever and ever!' (Revelation 11:15; 17:14).

Perfect peace

Fourthly, heaven is characterised by perfect peace. Un-clouded mutual love can only result in peaceful society (21:25-26). The fact that 'the gates shall not be shut at all by day' tells us that there is no threat. There are no locks on heaven's doors! Why? Because 'there is no night there'. This is literally true, for God's glory is never switched off. Who goes to bed if he is neither tired nor ill? It is only our present frailty in a fallen world that makes sleep neces-sary. Just as the God who watches over his people neither slumbers nor sleeps, so the saints in heaven will be eternally and tirelessly active. Spiritually, 'no night' implies 'no sin'. There will be no night in our experience of heaven, either in our relationships with others or in our own hearts and minds. 'The sin which we have as believers', notes Maurice Roberts, 'will be eradicated from our natures at every con-ceivable level'.[3]

Comprehensive godliness

Fifthly, there will be comprehensive godliness. There will be nothing in heaven that 'defiles, or causes an abomination or a lie' (21:27). 'Unpardoned sinners will never be admitted ... merely formal Christians will knock on the door ... [and] find it shut. Those who imagined they would be safe ... without the wedding garment of Christ's righteousness will be found out and solemnly excluded'.[3] Only those will be admitted whose names are written in 'The Lamb's book of life' and 'have washed their robes and made them white in the blood of the Lamb' (Revelation 7:14) — those who have believed in Jesus as their Saviour, whose atoning death pays the penalty of sin, and who are made righteous in him with a righteousness not their own (Romans 10:3; Philippians 3:9).

The Shorter Catechism (Q.37) asks: 'What benefits do believers receive from Christ at death?' and replies: 'The souls of believers are at their death made perfect in holiness (Hebrews 12:23) ... [and] do immediately pass into glory (2 Corinthians 5:1,6,8; Philippians 1:23; Luke 23:43)'.[4]

Unbounded happiness

Sixthly, we shall enjoy unbounded happiness. Scripture reveals heaven to be a place of unbounded happiness and exhilarating joy (22:1-5). It is the reality of which worldly happiness is the temporary and illusory substitute. For one thing, all true human needs are met in heaven (22:1-2). The New Jerusalem has a river, streets and trees. The river flows with 'the water of life' and the trees are of the 'tree of life' bearing fruit and carrying leaves 'for the healing of the nations'. On a physical level, heaven affords every comfort and provision to delight both body and soul. But the symbolism goes deeper. The 'water of life' is the Holy Spirit (John 7:37-39; cf. 4:13-14). The 'tree of life' speaks of Eden and Adam's sin, and then of restoration in Christ. Again, all causes of distress are eliminated in heaven (22:3). There will be 'no more curse', because God and Christ rule in glory and we shall serve him without hindrance. Finally, all of God's people will glory in Christ in heaven (22:4-5). Life is lived in the presence of the Lord in happy fellowship with him.

> *Believers are reconciled to him —*
> *'they shall see his face'.*
> *Believers belong to him —*
> *'His name shall be on their foreheads'.*
> *Believers are taught by him —*
> *'the Lord God gives them light'.*
> *Believers rule with him —*
> *'they shall reign for ever and ever'.*

The gospel is for ever. Jesus saves for ever. New life in Christ is forever. Heaven is forever. But hell is also forever for those who steadfastly reject the Saviour. Hell will be the endless night of God-denying souls. The vision of heaven calls you to Christ. Christ calls you to himself, to repent of sin and flee to him in faith for forgiveness of sin and everlasting life — that you might become 'a chosen generation, a royal priesthood, a holy nation, his own special people, that you may proclaim the praises of him who called you out of darkness into his marvellous light' (1 Peter 2:9-10).

NOTES

[1] Quoted in J. Gerstner, *Jonathan Edwards on Heaven and Hell* (Soli Deo Gloria, 1998) p.11

[2] J. MacArthur, *The Glory of Heaven* (Crossway Books, 1998) p.110

[3] M. Roberts, *The Thought of God* (Banner of Truth, 1994) p.207
[4] *Westminster Shorter Catechism* (www.reformed.org/documents/WSC_frames.html) Q.37

*But you have come to Mount Zion
and to the city of the living God,
the heavenly Jerusalem,
to an innumerable company of angels,
to the general assembly and church of the
firstborn who are registered in heaven,
to God the Judge of all,
to the spirits of just men made perfect,
to Jesus the Mediator of the new covenant, and
to the blood of sprinkling that speaks better
things than that of Abel.*

(Hebrews 12:22-24)

7. JUST MEN MADE PERFECT

What will we be like in heaven? The visions in the Book of Revelation characteristically portray the redeemed as a static audience of worshippers in white robes, assembled before God's throne. These visions have generated the images so popular with cartoonists, of saints standing around on clouds strumming harps — hardly an inviting prospect! But the Revelation is more about how God's people get through this world and into heaven than how they live when they get there. For this, we have to look elsewhere in the Bible.

Like home

The Bible tells us most about how we will live in heaven when it focuses on how we should live in this world. For what we will be there is the goal and model for what we ought to be here. John MacArthur comments that 'Heaven will seem more like home than the dearest spot on earth.'[1] Thus we are challenged in Hebrews 12 to 'run with endurance the race that is set before us' here and now (v.1), on the ground that we have come to 'the heavenly Jerusalem' and 'the spirits of just men made perfect' (v.23). Our destiny in eternity informs our calling in this present age. We are told what we will be like in the next life, so that we will know how — and why — to live in this life.

Our destination

There is no richer description in Scripture of what it will mean to live in heaven than Hebrews 12:22-24, which sets out the essential identity of God's believing people. Believers are heaven-born and heaven-bound. So when the writer to the Hebrews wants to help us live successfully, he points us to our goal, to heaven, and says, 'Be what you really are in Christ'.

To what, then, have we already come? The answer in Hebrews 12:22 is, perhaps, surprising. It is not about faithful church-going or successful Christian parenting. It is not about anything we do here. It is about heaven, angels, saved sinners, a new covenant, and a blood-bought salvation through a Mediator, Jesus, who loved us and gave himself for us. We have 'come to' heaven, and that gives meaning and direction to our discipleship in this world.

Made perfect

To understand what Christians will be like in heaven, however, we must focus on just one aspect of the 'heaven' to which we have already come, namely, 'the spirits of just men made perfect'. This refers to the present 'intermediate state' of the saved in heaven as they await the day of Jesus' Second Coming to this world. This state will continue only until believers are clothed with their resurrection bodies at the general resurrection. Nevertheless, it provides a window on our eternal state in the consummated new heavens and new earth.

The key is the term 'made perfect'. Even now the 'spirits' (souls without bodies) of 'just men' (believers declared righteous in Christ) are 'made perfect' (sanctified entirely, or glorified; Romans 8:30). This tells us that in passing from here to heaven, the believer is perfected in his soul. Nothing is left that could defile or exclude him from glory.

Our transformation

Fundamental transformations have already occurred in the believer. Already there is a new heart — 'a heart of flesh' in place of 'a heart of stone' (Ezekiel 36:26). Everyone who is 'in Christ' is 'a new creation; old things have passed away; behold all things have become new' (2 Corinthians 5:17). Even so, the choicest Christians are far from perfect. 'If we say that we have no sin, we deceive ourselves, and the truth is not in us' (1 John 1:8). We often feel the need of deliverance from 'this body of death' (Romans 7:25). This final deliverance is only going to be effected on the doorstep of glory, and has several aspects.

Perfected nature

In this life Christians are imperfect. Paul contrasts our present and future states when he writes: 'But we all ... beholding as in a mirror the glory of the Lord, are being transformed into the same image from glory to glory, just as by the Spirit of the Lord' (2 Corinthians 3:18). When Moses descended from Sinai, he veiled his face to conceal the reflected glory of God. Under the gospel, believers already have 'unveiled faces', which shine with spiritual radiance in Christ. But the day is coming when they will be taken from 'glory to glory'. They will be transformed to be like Christ, sharing his perfected human nature with unparalleled fullness: 'we shall be like him, for we shall see him as he is' (1 John 3:2).

Perfected behaviour

Christians are already regarded by God as cleansed and completely forgiven (1 Corinthians 6:9-11). They really know something of what it means for Christ to dwell in them, as 'the hope of glory' (Colossians 1:27; Romans 8:18). But Jesus prays for us to grow in grace and be sanctified through the Word of God (John 17:17). To be reckoned holy in a legal sense is one thing, but to be perfectly holy in every moment of daily life is something else again.

How, then, is our personal behaviour brought to perfection? Not by our efforts, which are compromised by daily sinning in thought, word and deed. Nor by 'doing time' in some unscriptural purgatory! But only by Jesus Christ our Saviour who, having justified his people, makes them perfectly holy, bringing them instantaneously to heaven (see Revelation 21:27). He frees us from evil and corruption in all its forms and gives us his perfect righteousness in its place.

Perfected bodies

The death of our physical body is tangible proof of our corruption and need of redemption. The resurrection promises a radically renewed body: 'sown in corruption, it is raised in incorruption ... sown in dishonour, it is raised in glory ... sown in weakness, it is raised in power ... sown a natural body, it is raised a spiritual body'. And the underlying reason for this is that 'as we have borne the image of the man of dust, we shall also bear the image of the heavenly Man' (1 Corinthians 15:42-44, 49). Here is the fulfilment of the psalmist's hope: 'I will see your face in righteousness; I shall be satisfied when I awake in your likeness' (Psalm 17:15).

Perfected enjoyment

Everybody wants to 'enjoy life', but all are not agreed as to
what 'enjoy' means. Yet all agree that life is less enjoyable
when bad things happen to us! Disappointments, illnesses,
betrayals, poverty, drudgery — the list is endless. But worst
of all is death. Yet death is the last hurdle between those
who love Jesus Christ and the perfect enjoyment of God
for ever in glory! At death every believer will hear God's
welcome: 'enter into the joy of your Lord' (Matthew 25:23),
and savour the 'fullness of joy' and 'pleasures for evermore'
that await us in his presence (Psalm 16:11).

Perfected relationships

How different life would be if we all
loved one another perfectly! Many will
dismiss the very notion as a fantasy. They
have a keen nose for the faults of others.
But Jesus' half-brother James had it all
pegged long ago: 'Where do wars and
fights come from among you? Do they
not come from your desires for pleasure
that war in your members?' (James 4:1-7). Heaven sees an
end to all strife, tears and broken relationships. Freedom
from sin means freedom to be holy. And perfected godliness
means perfected relationships. Family feuds, personality
clashes and doctrinal controversies will vanish for ever. All
will be cleansed of every fault and persuaded of every truth
and all will love one another in glorious harmony. Perfectly

sanctified hearts will rejoice in 'the unity of the Spirit and the bond of peace' without a shadow of disharmony.

Perfected fellowship with God

What makes fellowship with God possible is his initiative in reaching out to save lost sinners. The first prerequisite of fellowship, then, has to be the Lord's pleasure in those he has saved. Isaiah prophesied that God would 'see of the travail of [Christ's] soul, and be satisfied' (Isaiah 53:11). The obstacle to reconciliation — and therefore to fellowship — was removed at the cross.

The 'glorious church' (Ephesians 5:27) in heaven will be characterised by perfect fellowship with God in Christ her Saviour. Believers will be with Jesus (John 17:24). They will enjoy fellowship with the Father and the Son (1 John 1:3). They will have a full knowledge of the Lord (1 Corinthians 13:12) and they will see Jesus' face (Revelation 22:4). Their communion with God will be direct, visible, audible and perfect. All things are made new.

Our preparation

We said at the outset that what we will be in heaven is the goal and model for what we ought to be here. This brings us back to Hebrews 12. Our preparation for heaven is to 'run with endurance the race set before us' right now! — looking to Jesus, who brought us to saving faith (vv. 1-2); 'looking diligently lest anyone fall short of the grace of God' (v. 15); and seeing that we 'do not refuse him who speaks ... For our God is a consuming fire' (vv. 25,29).

NOTES

[1]J. MacArthur, *The Glory of Heaven* (Crossway Books, 1998) pp. 140-141

His lord said to him,
'Well done, good and faithful servant:
you were faithful over a few things,
I will make you ruler over many things.
Enter into the joy of your lord.'

(Matthew 25:21)

8. THE JOY OF THE LORD

Jesus' parable of the talents (Matthew 25:14-30) demonstrates that the way we choose to live now, relates to where we will spend eternity. The servants that are 'good and faithful' are handsomely rewarded, while the 'unprofitable servant', who sits on his hands, loses everything he had. It is a picture of faith and unbelief, and their consequences in time and eternity. The stark realities of the last judgement are set before us. But there is also a jewel here — the Lord's words to the faithful servants: 'Enter into the joy of your Lord' (vv. 21, 23). Notice that the joy gained is not ours but the Lord's. This opens up a startling and profound truth — the believer's happiness in heaven is not just his own sense of fulfilment, but participation in the happiness of God himself.

Joy from the Lord

What is the Lord's joy? It is first his joy in himself. The God who 'is love' (1 John 4:8) is possessed of 'fulness of joy' (Psalm 16:11). It is also his joy in loving — and saving to himself (Luke 15:10) — a people who were 'not a people' (1 Peter 2:10). He 'delights' in his people and in their godliness (Numbers 14:8; Deuteronomy 10:15; Proverbs 11:1,20; 12:22). He enjoys their love for him and their fellowship with him in worship and prayer (Proverbs 15:8; Jeremiah 9:24). Furthermore, this joy comes from union with Christ. It is the joy of one to whom they bear a personal relationship by a living faith.

What does it mean to 'enter' the Lord's joy? Thomas Boston observes that our joy in heaven will be 'pure and unmixed, without any dregs of sorrow; nor slight and momentary, but solid and everlasting, without interruption'. He continues: 'joy shall not only enter into us, but we shall enter into it, and swim forever in an ocean of joy, where we shall see nothing but joy wherever we turn ... Happy they that now sow in tears, which will spring up in joy in heaven, and will encircle their heads with a weight of glory'.[1]

Limitless joy

The psalmist's 'fulness of joy' (Psalm 16:11) is full not just because it fills us, but because it is God's joy. He offers three vital insights into heaven.

1. Heaven is joyous because God is there. It is, writes Edward Donnelly, 'above all ... a place of happiness'.[2] David begins Psalm 16 with a prayer for preservation but quickly rises to a glorious crescendo celebrating the joy of heaven: 'In your presence is fulness of joy; at your right hand are pleasures forevermore' (Psalm 16:11).

2. Heaven is joyous because God saves lost and dead people. David anticipates being there, alive from the dead: 'You will not leave my soul in Sheol, nor will you allow your Holy One to see corruption' (Psalm 16:10). The apostle Peter, preaching on the day of Pentecost, shows that David was here speaking ultimately of Christ and the resurrection (Acts 2:25-33). Nevertheless it was and is all about how sinners are saved by God's grace from spiritual and physical death. Unlike Jesus, we certainly do see corruption. But we will be raised to incorruptible glory in him (1 Corinthians 15:42-44).

3. Heaven is every believer's present happiness. David's 'heart is glad', his 'glory rejoices' and his 'flesh also will

rest in hope'. The hope of heaven energises his daily life. Christians already enjoy something of heaven! Without the hope of heaven, all our joys would be earth-bound and therefore inevitably fleeting. This is exactly the sadness that blights those with no heavenly hope, because they believe that the best they can know is what they experience now, while they live. That is also why so many are so concerned about their 'legacy' — what they leave behind — whether it is some lasting accomplishment, a revered memory, a name on a building, or a place in history. But that is all about the past. The hope of heaven is about the future, and it carries past and present into that future on the wings of salvation received in Christ.

We already know the difference between 'treasures on earth' and 'treasures in heaven' (Matthew 6:19-20), but not the fulness of God's blessings. Presently, we experience great comfort from the Lord — 'the oil of joy for mourning' and 'the garment of praise for the spirit of heaviness' (Isaiah 61:3). But only in heaven will there be 'no more tears' (Revelation 21:4). Now, 'we behold as in a mirror the glory of the Lord' (2 Corinthians 3:18). But only in heaven will we see Jesus 'face to face' (1 Corinthians 13:12).

Joy from now on

We enter into the joy of the Lord by exercising faith in Jesus Christ. Christians should be the happiest people in the world, since they know what it is to be saved. They should be full of love and thanksgiving to the Lord who bought

Gordon J. Keddie

HEAVEN

HEAVEN

CONTENTS

page

Author's Preface

Most people like to believe there is a heaven — and that they will go there when they die. An ABC News poll in December 2005 found that 89% of all Americans believe in heaven and 75% expect to make it there. However, only 21% think you need to be a Christian (these are probably the Evangelicals) and just 22% of all who believe in heaven think we will have a body when we get there (that is, not all Evangelicals are clear on the resurrection of the body).

There has long been confusion (and presumption) on this topic. All religions have their versions of heaven and how to get there. Our multicultural interfaith world expects us to be accepting of everybody's views and not to press the exclusive claims of the only authoritative source on the subject that exists — the Bible.

But for every single person the day is coming when the truth will be revealed — when presumptuous certainties and vapid uncertainties will alike be tested and found wanting. God's Word is quite clear that there is salvation in no name under heaven save that of Jesus Christ (Acts 4:12). It also tells us a fair bit about heaven and a great deal about how to get there. 'God so loved the world that he gave his only begotten Son, that whoever believes in him should not perish but have everlasting life' (John 3:16). This little book seeks to point the way.

Gordon J. Keddie
Indianapolis, USA
January 2006

1. THINKING ABOUT HEAVEN

Do you think much about heaven? The Bible is full of eternity and constantly points us to the last judgement and the great divide between heaven and hell.

God has 'put eternity' in our hearts (Ecclesiastes 3:11) and he calls us to think seriously about where we will spend it. He sent his only-begotten Son to save his people from their sins and bring to heaven 'a great multitude which no one could number of all tribes, peoples and tongues' (Revelation 7:9).

Plan A or plan B?

Scripture refers to 'heaven' some 600 times. The New Testament is replete with references to the hope of heaven and the goal of glory, through saving faith in Jesus Christ. Yet heaven is given little thought, even by Christians. We often treat it like social security — something that will be there when we need it. In theory it is our goal, but in practice it is God's 'Plan B' for our lives. Meanwhile we stick with 'Plan A' (enjoying this life) for as long as possible.

Some, of course, reject the hope of heaven as so much 'pie-in-the-sky-by-and-by'. A. E. Housman's poem 'Ho Everyone that Thirsteth', takes its title from Isaiah 55:1 and alludes to John 7:37 and Ecclesiastes 12:5 but wearily proceeds to dismiss the teaching of the Scriptures as essentially unbelieveable and undesirable. He writes:

> *Ho everyone that thirsteth*
> *And hath the price to give,*
> *Come to the stolen waters,*
> *Drink and your soul shall live*

They buy into the idea that you can be 'so heavenly-minded that you're no earthly use'. Heaven is just not very practical. Never mind that Scripture teaches the very opposite!

2. 'Heaven is boring'. We accept the cartoon caricature — folks in white robes with halos, sitting on clouds and playing harps for ever: even more tedious, some might say, than going to church for a million years!

3. 'Heaven is too hard to think about. Where is it? How does it work? What do you do? How do you get there? Yes, Jesus went up to heaven but it is hard to understand how. Besides, we have too much to do right here and now. Let's think about it later!

The real problem

The real problem, of course, is none of the above. It is that we are too tied to this life. The rich man in Jesus' story in Luke 12:16-21 is a classic case (more on this later; see chapter 9). He was too busy getting rich to think of either heaven or hell or even God himself. It is only too easy to 'walk by sight' when we should 'walk by faith' (2 Corinthians 5:7). We are alive, we are healthy and we have a life to live. In spite of all its problems, this world is a great place and what it offers really appeals to us.

Death and eternity seem far away — that is, until the day comes (as it will) when, like the rich fool, we will hear God say: 'This night your soul will be required of you' (Luke 12:20). If even Christians think this way, how much more the unconverted? To them the claims of Jesus are offensive and the prospects of facing a righteous Judge are just too awful to contemplate. It is small wonder that, like the rich fool in Jesus' parable, millions just put up the shutters of find that belief in universal salvation is the norm. Dead celebrities (if we are to believe the tearful testimonies of their friends) are watching us benignly from heaven, however unbelieving or immoral their past lives. If singing *The Lord's my Shepherd* at funerals conveyed grace to dead sinners, no one would ever be lost! It begs the question people don't want to ask about the departed one: 'Was the Lord Jesus Christ his Shepherd?' Do the comforts of Psalm 23 apply to all and sundry — whatever they believe and however they live their lives? The answer of God's Word is too painfully obvious. But people will cling to false hopes rather than cling to Christ himself.

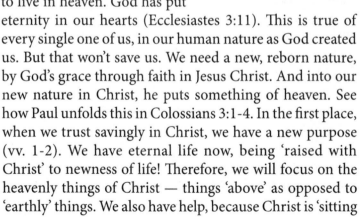

Live and grow

Are you already a Christian? Then understand that you will never be more fit to live on earth, than when you are fit to live in heaven. God has put eternity in our hearts (Ecclesiastes 3:11). This is true of every single one of us, in our human nature as God created us. But that won't save us. We need a new, reborn nature, by God's grace through faith in Jesus Christ. And into our new nature in Christ, he puts something of heaven. See how Paul unfolds this in Colossians 3:1-4. In the first place, when we trust savingly in Christ, we have a new purpose (vv. 1-2). We have eternal life now, being 'raised with Christ' to newness of life! Therefore, we will focus on the heavenly things of Christ — things 'above' as opposed to 'earthly' things. We also have help, because Christ is 'sitting

1 Corinthians 2:9-10, quoting Isaiah 64:4 and 65:17: 'Eye has not seen, nor ear heard, nor have entered into the heart of man the things which God has prepared for those who love him.' But he does not stop with this statement of relative ignorance. He continues: 'But God has revealed them to us through his Spirit. For the Spirit searches all things, yes, the deep things of God.' Alive in Christ, and walking in the Spirit, we are called and equipped to be so heavenly-minded that we will be of great earthly use. We need to know more of heaven, more of glory, more of Christ. Let us then seek — and set our minds on — things above, where Christ is. Then we will live and labour in Christ's kingdom here, as those whose home is heaven.

NOTES

1 Quoted in F. Kermode (ed.) *The Oxford Anthology of English Literature Vol. II* (Oxford University Press, 1973) p.2035

2. OUR FATHER IS IN HEAVEN

In his letter to the Colossians, the apostle Paul challenges us to set our minds 'on things above, not things on the earth' (Colossians 3:1-4). The great motive for being truly heavenly-minded is that the believer is 'raised with Christ'. He has a new and everlasting life through faith in Jesus as his Saviour. Paul also reminds us that the risen Christ is even now in heaven, 'sitting at the right hand of God'. He is located there with our humanity, exalted as Lord and 'head over all things to the church' (Ephesians 1:22).

The Father

In thinking about Jesus' heavenly glory, we can easily forget the fact that God the Father is also there. Jesus is, after all, at the right hand of the Father. Indeed, it is the presence of the Father that defines Jesus' glory (John 17:5). You see this in Psalm 16:11 where David, in the language of prophecy, records Christ saying to the Father: 'In your presence is fullness of joy: at your right hand are pleasures forevermore'. The Father is the definition of glory, the source of joy forever and ever. The same thing is found in the Lord's Prayer, which begins: 'Our Father in heaven ...' (Matthew 6:9). I dare say that when we pray these words, we are so focused on the person of the Father, as the one who hears prayer (Psalm 65:1-2), that we hardly think of *where* he is. Our Father is 'in heaven'. He is not portrayed as being elsewhere or everywhere. It is from somewhere called heaven that his omnipresence reaches out into every corner of his creation.

from the heavens above us.

although it clearly exists on an altogether different plane

Heaven is for Christians

Scripture assures us that Christians 'have a building from God, a house not made with hands, eternal in the heavens' (2 Corinthians 5:1). This contrasts with 'our earthly house, this tent', our mortal body which is 'destroyed' by death. Paul's point is that we will have bodies in heaven — resurrection bodies. Heaven must therefore be a created place where saved sinners and unfallen angels will live in the presence of the glorious God and the exalted Christ. Yet the immensity of God means that 'heaven and the heaven of heavens cannot contain [him]' (1 Kings 8:27). What a marvellous condescension to finite human beings it is, then, that the infinite God should manifest his glory in a place designed and adapted for everlasting human habitation — 'a new heavens and a new earth' (Isaiah 65:17; 66:22). The earth and the first two heavens will be reconstituted in what is now the third heaven, that the new humanity in Christ may be gloriously consummated in a new creation where 'righteousness dwells' (2 Peter 3:13).

Heaven is where Jesus reigns

Heaven is where Christians will be forever because the Lord Jesus Christ is there with his Father. First of all, Jesus is exalted in heaven to rule as sovereign over this world in the interests of his people. The Father's acceptance of Jesus' perfect sacrifice for sin guarantees his acceptance of those for whom Christ died and secures their salvation in time and eternity (Philippians 2:9-11; Ephesians 1:20-23; Hebrews 1:1-3; 1 Peter 3:22). Secondly, Jesus is preparing

your heart be also'(Matthew 6:19-23).
Where is your heart? Is it set on heaven
or rooted in this world?

We are promised that as we follow
the Lord, he will guide us in life and
bring us to heaven. Paul tells Timothy how to persevere in a faithful life,
especially when buffeted by sufferings
for the faith. He says: 'For this reason I
also suffer these things; nevertheless I
am not ashamed, for I know whom I have believed and am
persuaded that he is able to keep what I have committed
to him until that Day' (2 Timothy 1:12). He does not cling
to some hope of earthly relief or success, but anchors his
confidence in the Day of Christ's return and his consummation of the gospel of the kingdom. Heaven is the great
goal, not some earthly glory.

In Psalm 73:23-24, Asaph agonises over the challenge
of living for God in an evil world, where the wicked seem to
enjoy successful lives and easy deaths. He found the answer,
of course, in terms of eternity — of sin, judgement and
salvation. Accordingly, he praises the Lord as his Father in
heaven and looks forward to the glory yet to be revealed:

> *Yet evermore I am with thee:*
> *Thou holdest me by my right hand.*
> *And thou, ev'n thou, my guide shalt be;*
> *Thy counsel shall my way command;*
> *And afterward in glory bright*
> *Shalt thou receive me to thy sight.*

NOTES

[1] L. Berkhof, *Systematic Theology* (Banner of Truth, 1957) p.737 [Berkhof
devotes one page of 738 to the subject of heaven].

3. A BUILDING FROM GOD

One of the most searching challenges in the Bible is surely Solomon's charge to young people in Ecclesiastes 12. He first says: 'Remember your Creator in the days of your youth, before the difficult days come, and the years draw near when you say, I have no pleasure in them' (12:1). He then describes in relentless detail the progressive loss of faculties in old age — no less powerfully for the poetic language — until 'man goes to his eternal home, and the mourners go about the streets' (vv. 3-5). It is a simple and unanswerable argument. Our bodies are wearing out, our 'spirit' will soon return to God who gave it, and we urgently need to turn to God (vv. 7, 13-14). How we respond to this challenge will determine where we spend eternity and how we spend the rest of our lives.

Responding to realities

Sometimes people react with anger. Sometimes they respond by denying the obvious, trying hard not to think of death and eternity. They try to 'live life to the full' as if this life will never come to a reckoning, either in time or eternity. What a liberation it is, however, to accept both God's diagnosis and cure! To accept that our 'outward man' is perishing but that, through faith in Jesus Christ as Saviour, the 'inward man' is renewed day by day, even in the face of physical decline (2 Corinthians 4:16). But Paul does not leave the matter there. He looks beyond death and into eternity: 'For we know that if our earthly house, this tent, is destroyed, we have a building from God, a house not made with hands, eternal in the heavens' (2 Corinthians 5:1ff).

kind of thing. Why? Because they underestimate their own corruption and they underestimate the glory of heaven. Heaven, however, is a lot more that just being alive in our present bodies, minus illnesses and physical defects. Things will be different in heaven, for 'the Lord Jesus Christ ... will transform our lowly body [to] be conformed to his glorious body' (Philippians 3:21). We shall be changed and 'further clothed, that mortality may be swallowed up by life' (v. 4).

Clothed

In a passage of striking brilliance, A. A. Hodge likens this transformation to the instantaneous restoration of sight and hearing to one born blind and deaf: 'Some such experience will be yours and mine when we are clothed upon with our glorified bodies on the morning of the resurrection. Coming up from rural and urban graveyards, rising before the awful whiteness of the throne and the intolerable glory of him that sits thereon, and passing through the interminable ranks of flaming seraphs and diademed archangels, the perfect senses of our new bodies will bring us at once into the presence of the whole universe, of the music of all its spheres, and of the effulgence of all its suns — of the most secret working of all its forces, and of the recorded history of all its past'.[2]

Neither does Paul follow Plato's idea of the body as a

because 'we walk by faith, not by sight' (v. 7). The Christian is more impressed by what he believes than by what he sees. He looks in the mirror and sees his days ebbing away. He looks to Christ by faith and sees everlasting glory. As he 'walks' by faith, his hope in God's promise is enlarged and his experience of God's grace deepened. Does this touch your experience today and every day? I rather fear that many Christians are afraid to leave this body, this life and this world to be with the Lord. But if we truly love Christ we will desire to be with him.

Living for God

Thirdly, there is a practical programme. Earnest longing for heaven is the engine that powers effective living on earth. It negates the 'too heaven-ly minded, no earthly use' idea, and the claim of secular culture that 'this world is all there is'. Many Christians unwittingly 'buy into' these worldly attitudes. They neither hope actively for heaven, nor relate to heaven as they live in the world. Paul therefore delineates the heaven-focused discipleship that makes for practical Christian living. First comes commitment to pleasing God (v. 9). The starting point of godly behaviour is the consideration that one day we shall be present with the Lord. It follows that whether 'present or absent' we seek to be 'well pleasing to him'. Further motivation comes from the conviction that we are accountable to Christ. We must

NOTES

[1] E. Donnelly, *Heaven and Hell* (Banner of Truth, 2002) p.108

[2] A. A. Hodge, *Evangelical Theology* (Banner of Truth, 1996) p.380

transformation is summarised in a startling way by John's declaration that 'there was no more sea'. Hendriksen points out: 'At present the sea is the emblem of unrest and conflict. The roaring, raging, agitated, tempest-tossed waters, the waves perpet- ually engaged in combat with one another symbolise the nations of the world in their conflict and unrest.'[2] For example, Isaiah says 'the wicked are like the troubled sea, when it

cannot rest, whose waters cast up mire and dirt' (Isaiah 57:20). John Martin (1789-1854), a British artist well known for his apocalyptic canvases, painted 'The Plains of Heaven' to illustrate Revelation 21. It is in the Tate Gallery in London. A fleet of gondolas is bringing the redeemed to the shore of a great lake, to be met by angels in white robes. The holy city is supposedly descending in the clouds and the landscape is vast and beautiful, filled with flowers, the cedars of Lebanon, and the palm trees of Elim. There is no sun, but light suffuses everything. There is no more sea, but rivers and lakes abound. This is not your standard angels-with-harps-on-a-cloud cartoon, but one man's seri- ous attempt to evoke something of the renewed world of the glory to come.

under the burden imposed by human sin and be 'delivered from the bondage of corruption into the glorious liberty of the children of God' (Romans 8:20-22). Our present defiled environment will become the new environment in which God's people will live for ever. There will be no Chernobyls, no Love Canals, and no Exxon Valdez's in the 'new heaven and the new earth'.

A recreated city

John also sees a recreated city (21:2, 9-21), a 'new Jerusalem' descending from heaven from God. This 'holy city' is represented as already existing. It descends from heaven as it presently is, so as to become the centre-piece of the new earth. The expression 'holy city' reaches back to the 'Salem' of Melchizedek, who prefigured Christ (Hebrews 7:1-21). It relates to David's Jerusalem, where God presenced himself in the Temple, and to Mount Zion, which in Scripture represents the church as the people of God (Galatians 4:26-28; Hebrews 12:22). The centrality of Jerusalem to the Old Testament church is expressed in the lament of the exiled Jews in Babylon: 'If I forget you, O Jerusalem, let my right hand forget its skill! If I do not remember you, let my tongue cling to the roof of my mouth — if I do not exalt Jerusalem above my chief joy' (Psalm 137:5). 'Among the many illustrations that convey the nature of heaven to us', observes E. M. Bounds, 'the illustration of a city is the most striking ... A city teems with life in its richest and most strenuous form. It has never felt the chill of death ... Graves have never been dug there ... Heaven is a city of life ... Heaven knows no tears and has never felt a sorrow. It is filled with eternal, brilliant and vibrant life'.[4]

A city full of believing people

Who will inhabit heaven? The vision provides its own answer. The inhabitants will be those who are 'the bride' of Christ (v. 2). The fact that

the gates of the city are named for the twelve tribes of Israel, and the foundations of the walls for the twelve apostles (vv. 12-14), indicates that a redeemed citizenry is in view, that is, those whose names 'are written in the Lamb's book of life' (v. 27). This is confirmed by three distinct emphases in the passage, the last of which is a call to people of every era to repent of sin and believe in the Lord. Firstly, God comes to us for ever: 'God himself will be with them and be their God' (v. 3). The relationship between God and (the new) humanity is resolved completely and permanently by his unhindered presence and fellowship with them. They, for their part, are reconciled through 'the blood of the everlasting covenant' in Jesus Christ (Hebrews 13:20).

Secondly, God saves us from all evil, and salvation comes to its final victory: 'God will wipe away every tear ... [and] make all things new' (vv. 4-5). The condition of God's people will be resolved fully and permanently by the removal of all the effects of sin and its corruption. There will be no death, sorrow, crying or pain. Thirdly, God calls us to account even now (vv. 6-8). The application is that every one of us is accountable to the sovereign God right now. On which side of God's victory will you end up? As we might expect in a vision of the final consummation of God's

Eternal destiny

Finally, God reminds us of the default destination for those
who will not repent (v. 8). The unrepentant and unbelieving
will be 'turned into hell' (Psalm 9:17). This is the 'second
death' — the unending state of spiritual deadness under
God's righteous judgement. This is a sombre note on which
to end a section on how all things are to be made new. The
drama of the moment, however, has the clear intent of underlining the urgency of the issue for every living human
being. The coming of Christ, and the revealing of the new
heaven and new earth, may yet be long delayed in terms
of human history. But the eternal destiny of those who are
alive today will be settled in a very short time (anything
from minutes to decades!) This is a blink of God's eye. If
we have any sense at all, we must know that the moment
of decision is upon us. We must close with Christ and
embrace him as our Saviour. Peter urges us to make the
proper application in our lives: 'Therefore, since all these
will be dissolved, what manner of persons ought you to be
in holy conduct and godliness, looking for and hastening
the coming of the day of God, because of which the heavens will be dissolved, being on fire, and the elements will
melt with fervent heat? Nevertheless we, according to his
promise, look for new heavens and a new earth in which
righteousness dwells' (2 Peter 3:11-13).

NOTES

[1] J. MacArthur, *The Glory of Heaven* (Crossway Books, 1998) pp. 107-
108
[2] *Westminster Shorter Catechism* (www.reformed.org/documents/WSC_
frames.html) Q.1

6. THE EXPERIENCE OF HEAVEN

What will heaven be like? We have already seen, in Revelation 21: 1-21, something of what we called 'the geography of glory' — what heaven will look like when this world is wound up at 'the end of the age' (Matthew 13:49; 24:3; 28:20). But now the focus changes to the experience of glory — what it will be like to live in that new heaven and new earth as the saved, sanctified and glorified people of God.

Vision

We must again remember that this is a vision and not a video. Jonathan Edwards comments: 'There is nothing upon earth that will suffice to represent to us the glory of heaven.'[1] The glimpses of glory that God gave in the past — for example, to Moses on Sinai and to the disciples at Jesus' transfiguration — all point to something far greater, namely, the glory of heaven. The visions of heaven and the holy city represent realities which will not only be seen and felt, but which will transcend all the foretastes given us in Scripture and the most spectacular sights we have seen in this present world. Heaven will be a feast for the senses and the soul, and excite our wonder for all eternity.

Our passage reveals something of what it means to be 'partakers of the inheritance of the saints in light' (Colossians 1:12). It unfolds six particular qualities of that experience.

or a lie' (21:27). 'Unpardoned sinners will never be admitted ... merely formal Christians will knock on the door ... [and] find it shut. Those who imagined they would be safe ... without the wedding garment of Christ's righteousness will be found out and solemnly excluded'.[3] Only those will be admitted whose names are written in 'The Lamb's book of life' and 'have washed their robes and made them white in the blood of the Lamb' (Revelation 7:14) — those who have believed in Jesus as their Saviour, whose atoning death pays the penalty of sin, and who are made righteous in him with a righteousness not their own (Romans 10:3; Philippians 3:9).

The Shorter Catechism (Q.37) asks: 'What benefits do believers receive from Christ at death?' and replies: 'The souls of believers are at their death made perfect in holiness (Hebrews 12:23) ... [and] do immediately pass into glory (2 Corinthians 5:1,6,8; Philippians 1:23; Luke 23:43)'.[4]

Unbounded happiness

Sixthly, we shall enjoy unbounded happiness. Scripture reveals heaven to be a place of unbounded happiness and exhilarating joy (22:1-5). It is the reality of which worldly happiness is the temporary and illusory substitute. For one thing, all true human needs are met in heaven (22:1-2). The New Jerusalem has a river, streets and trees. The river flows with 'the water of life' and the trees are of the 'tree of life' bearing fruit and carrying leaves 'for the healing of the nations'. On a physical level, heaven affords every comfort and provision to delight both body and soul. But the symbolism goes deeper. The 'water of life' is the Holy Spirit (John 7:37-39; cf. 4:13-14). The 'tree of life' speaks

[3] M. Roberts, *The Thought of God* (Banner of Truth, 1994) p.207
[4] *Westminster Shorter Catechism* (www.reformed.org/documents/WSC_frames.html) Q.37

7. Just men made perfect

What will we be like in heaven? The visions in the Book of Revelation characteristically portray the redeemed as a static audience of worshippers in white robes, assembled before God's throne. These visions have generated the images so popular with cartoonists, of saints standing around on clouds strumming harps — hardly an inviting prospect! But the Revelation is more about how God's people get through this world and into heaven than how they live when they get there. For this, we have to look elsewhere in the Bible.

Like home

The Bible tells us most about how we will live in heaven when it focuses on how we should live in this world. For what we will be there is the goal and model for what we ought to be here. John MacArthur comments that 'Heaven will seem more like home than the dearest spot on earth'.[1] Thus we are challenged in Hebrews 12 to 'run with endurance the race that is set before us' here and now (v.1), on the ground that we have come to 'the heavenly Jerusalem' and 'the spirits of just men made perfect' (v.23). Our destiny in eternity informs our calling in this present age. We are told what we will be like in the next life, so that we will know how — and why — to live in this life.

Our destination

There is no richer description in Scripture of what it will mean to live in heaven than Hebrews 12:22-24, which sets be satisfied when I awake in your likeness' (Psalm 17:15).

Perfected enjoyment

Everybody wants to 'enjoy life', but all are not agreed as to what 'enjoy' means. Yet all agree that life is less enjoyable when bad things happen to us! Disappointments, illnesses, betrayals, poverty, drudgery — the list is endless. But worst of all is death. Yet death is the last hurdle between those who love Jesus Christ and the perfect enjoyment of God for ever in glory! At death every believer will hear God's welcome: 'enter into the joy of your Lord' (Matthew 25:23), and savour the 'fullness of joy' and 'pleasures for evermore' that await us in his presence (Psalm 16:11).

Perfected relationships

How different life would be if we all loved one another perfectly! Many will dismiss the very notion as a fantasy. They have a keen nose for the faults of others. But Jesus' half-brother James had it all pegged long ago: 'Where do wars and fights come from among you? Do they not come from your desires for pleasure that war in your members?' (James 4:1-7). Heaven sees an end to all strife, tears and broken relationships. Freedom from sin means freedom to be holy. And perfected godliness means perfected relationships. Family feuds, personality clashes and doctrinal controversies will vanish for ever. All will be cleansed of every fault and persuaded of every truth and all will love one another in glorious harmony. Perfectly

8. The joy of the Lord

Jesus' parable of the talents (Matthew 25:14-30) demonstrates that the way we choose to live now, relates to where we will spend eternity. The servants that are 'good and faithful' are handsomely rewarded, while the 'unprofitable servant', who sits on his hands, loses everything he had. It is a picture of faith and unbelief, and their consequences in time and eternity. The stark realities of the last judgement are set before us. But there is also a jewel here — the Lord's words to the faithful servants: 'Enter into the joy of your Lord' (vv. 21, 23). Notice that the joy gained is not ours but the Lord's. This opens up a startling and profound truth — the believer's happiness in heaven is not just his own sense of fulfilment, but participation in the happiness of God himself.

Joy from the Lord

What is the Lord's joy? It is first his joy in himself. The God who 'is love' (1 John 4:8) is possessed of 'fulness of joy' (Psalm 16:11). It is also his joy in loving — and saving to himself (Luke 15:10) — a people who were 'not a people' (1 Peter 2:10). He 'delights' in his people and in their godliness (Numbers 14:8; Deuteronomy 10:15; Proverbs 11:1,20; 12:22). He enjoys their love for him and their fellowship with him in worship and prayer (Proverbs 15:8; Jeremiah 9:24). Furthermore, this joy comes from union with Christ. It is the joy of one to whom they bear a personal relationship by a living faith.

What does it mean to 'enter' the Lord's joy? Thomas Boston observes that our joy in heaven will be 'pure and

rest in hope.' The hope of heaven energises his daily life.
Christians already enjoy something of heaven! Without
the hope of heaven, all our joys would be earth-bound and
therefore inevitably fleeting. This is exactly the sadness that
blights those with no heavenly hope, because they believe
that the best they can know is what they experience now,
while they live. That is also why so many are so concerned
about their 'legacy' — what they leave behind — whether it
is some lasting accomplishment, a revered memory, a name
on a building, or a place in history. But that is all about the
past. The hope of heaven is about the future, and it carries
past and present into that future on the wings of salvation
received in Christ.

We already know the difference between 'treasures
on earth' and 'treasures in heaven' (Matthew 6:19-20), but
not the fulness of God's blessings. Presently, we experience
great comfort from the Lord — 'the oil of joy for mourning' and 'the garment of praise for the spirit of heaviness'
(Isaiah 61:3). But only in heaven will there be 'no more
tears' (Revelation 21:4). Now,' we behold as in a mirror
the glory of the Lord' (2
Corinthians 3:18). But only
in heaven will we see Jesus
'face to face' (1 Corinthians
13:12).

Joy from now on

We enter into the joy of the Lord by exercising faith in Jesus Christ. Christians should be the happiest people in the
world, since they know what it is to be saved. They should
be full of love and thanksgiving to the Lord who bought

3. *Exercise faith.* 'Without faith it is impossible to please God, for he who comes to God must believe that he is, and that he is a rewarder of those who diligently seek him' (Hebrews 11:6). If we want real joy, we must exercise real faith. Paul prays: 'Now may the God of hope fill you with all joy and peace in believing, that you may abound in hope by the power of the Holy Spirit' (Romans 15:13). Without 'believing' there can be no 'joy and peace'. Conversely, a living faith bears fruit, through the Spirit's ministry in our hearts. Joy and peace rise to an overflowing hope. It is 'by faith' in Jesus Christ — and through him alone — that we 'have access ... into this grace in which

we stand, and rejoice in hope of the glory of God' (Romans 5:1-2). Is that a description of your actual relationship to Christ? Commitment, passion and enthusiasm for the things of God? Anything less is a dangerous sham and will not bring a soul to heaven.

4. *Devote yourself to rejoicing in the Lord.* The Philippian Christians could 'rejoice always' because they have something about which to be joyful — salvation and the prospect of heaven.

Joy inexpressible

There is much besides. Psalm 148 calls us to praise the Lord for just about everything he has made: the heavens, the heights, the angels, the stars, the weather and the diversity of animal life in the world. But in the end the greatest cause them with his death on the cross. Christians are often sad when they see widespread blasphemy against God and the shipwreck of so many lives around them — whose present miseries are only a foretaste of worse to come, if they never turn to the Lord. So it is good and necessary to remember to 'rejoice in the Lord always' (Philippians 4:4). How can we do this? Let me suggest four ways.

1. *Be heavenly-minded.* We will never be heavenly-minded until our minds dwell on heavenly things (Colossians 3:1-4). Richard Baxter exhorts: 'Beloved friends, if we would but try this life with God, and would but keep these hearts above, what a spring of joy would be within us, and all our graces be fresh and green! How would the face of our souls be changed, and all that is within us rejoice ... O Christian, get above: believe it, that region is warmer than this below'.[3]

2. *Pray for more light.* 'Can you have comforts from God,' continues Baxter, 'and never think of him? Can heaven rejoice when you think not on it?' In Psalm 4, David reflects on how the Lord answers prayer, but notes that many still complain: 'Who will show us any good?' He answers this question by his own example. First comes a prayer: 'Lord, lift up the light of your countenance upon us'. Secondly, he testifies to his own experience of God's grace: 'You have put gladness in my heart'. Thirdly, he confesses his trust in the Lord: 'I will both lie down in peace and sleep; for you alone, O Lord, make me dwell in safety' (vv. 7-8). People often complain about 'the hand life has dealt them'. But will they turn to the Lord for salvation? Do they want to have hearts gladdened by his grace? If not, what expectation can they have of peace and safety, now or in eternity?

3. *Exercise faith*. 'Without faith it is impossible to please God, for he who comes to God must believe that he is, and that he is a rewarder of those who diligently seek him' (Hebrews 11:6). If we want real joy, we must exercise real faith. Paul prays: 'Now may the God of hope fill you with all joy and peace in believing, that you may abound in hope by the power of the Holy Spirit' (Romans 15:13). Without 'believing' there can be no 'joy and peace'. Conversely, a living faith bears fruit, through the Spirit's ministry in our hearts. Joy and peace rise to an overflowing hope. It is 'by faith' in Jesus Christ — and through him alone — that we 'have access ... into this grace in which

we stand, and rejoice in hope of the glory of God' (Romans 5:1-2). Is that a description of your actual relationship to Christ? Commitment, passion and enthusiasm for the things of God? Anything less is a dangerous sham and will not bring a soul to heaven.

4. *Devote yourself to rejoicing in the Lord.* The Philippian Christians could 'rejoice always' because they have something about which to be joyful — salvation and the prospect of heaven.

Joy inexpressible

There is much besides. Psalm 148 calls us to praise the Lord for just about everything he has made: the heavens, the heights, the angels, the stars, the weather and the diversity of animal life in the world. But in the end the greatest cause for rejoicing is God himself. Psalm 148 continues: 'Let them praise the name of the Lord, for his name alone is exalted: his glory is above the earth and heaven. And he has exalted the horn of his people, the praise of all his saints — of the children of Israel, a people near to him' (vv. 13-14). Believers rejoice in the Lord, because they are his, and it exalts their spirits and enlivens their hope of glory. 'Is not my assurance of being glorified one of these days,' asks Baxter, 'a sufficient ground of inexpressible joy?'[4]

I fear that too many of us are more sad about dying and leaving this earth, than we are happy about going to heaven to be forever with the Lord. Rejoicing always is a mandate from heaven, and it has heaven as its goal. It is the harbinger of our entrance into the joy of the Lord. And with it comes an unspoken invitation to share John's vision and joy. At the end of a long and fruitful life, and the ineffable insights of the Book of Revelation, he could say with joyous conviction: 'Even so, come, Lord Jesus! The grace of our Lord Jesus Christ be with you all. Amen' (Revelation 22:20-21).

NOTES

[1] T. Boston, *Human Nature in its Fourfold State* (Banner of Truth, 1964) pp. 460-461

[2] E. Donnelly, *Heaven and Hell* (Banner of Truth, 2001) p.110

[3] R. Baxter, *The Saints' Everlasting Rest* (Sovereign Grace Publishers, 2000) p.266

[4] R. Baxter, *The Saints' Everlasting Rest* (Sovereign Grace Publishers, 2000) p.315

And do this, knowing the time,
that now it is high time to awake out of sleep;
for now our salvation is nearer
than when we first believed.
The night is far spent, the day is at hand.
Therefore let us cast off the works of darkness,
and let us put on the armour of light.
Let us walk properly, as in the day,
not in revelry and drunkenness, not in lewdness
and lust, not in strife and envy.
But put on the Lord Jesus Christ,
and make no provision for the flesh,
to fulfill its lusts.

(Romans 13:11-14)

9. TIME TO WAKE UP!

The Bible confronts us with a vital question — are we in any condition to go to heaven? Scripture offers no encouragement for us to make assumptions about heaven. Peter tells us bluntly: 'if the righteous scarcely be saved, where shall the ungodly and the sinner appear?' (1 Peter 4:18). God keeps 'mercy for thousands, forgiving iniquity, transgression and sin', but he will by no means clear the guilty (Exodus 34:7).

Illusion

Most people who believe there is a God (of some kind) expect to go to a heaven (of some kind). It is often as vague as that. It has to be vague, because any serious reflection on the only source of information about heaven — the Bible — would quickly shoot down their airy presumptions and leave them shaking in their shoes (or, more likely, annoyed at God for being so particular).

Vaguely 'religious' folk instinctively know that God's Word will tell them things they would rather not know — that they don't especially love God, that they are not eager to keep his commandments, and that they feel little need of a Saviour (they are pretty decent folk, after all). They prefer the illusion of a heaven that costs nothing in the way of serious devotion to God and to his Son, the Lord Jesus Christ. That is why God tells everyone who has ears to hear, that it is 'high time to awake out of sleep'. We are dying people and ought to prepare for heaven. But that requires a living, trusting, committed faith in the Lord of glory, Jesus Christ.

Wake up!

I can still hear my Mum, every school-day morning, calling loudly: 'It's time to get up, boys!' But God's wake-up call says: 'Do this, knowing the time, that now it is high time to awaken out of sleep' (Romans 13:11). Consider three questions. Firstly, do you know what is going on? Every household has a daily timetable. When the alarm-clock goes off we know the time. God's world is also on a timetable, and this is his alarm going off! His plan of salvation is moving to its final consummation. 'It is the last epoch in this world's history', says John Murray.[1] The Bible calls it 'the last days' (Acts 2:17 etc.). The focus is on the 'glorious appearing of our great God and Saviour Jesus Christ' (Titus 2:13). Do you understand the times in which we live? Your answer will determine how you live life day by day, and whether you are prepared for death and eternity. Secondly, do you know where you are going? The call to 'awake out of sleep' prompts us to consider our destiny. God calls the unsaved to new life in Christ — 'Awake, you who sleep. Arise from the dead, and Christ will give you light' (Ephesians 5:14). But even believers tend to fall asleep spiritually. Even the wise virgins in the parable fell asleep (Matthew 25:5). The church in Ephesus left her first love (Revelation 2:3-4). Christians, therefore, need to work at being what they already are in Christ — awakened souls. 'But you, brethren', says Paul, 'are not in darkness so that this Day should overtake you as a thief ... Therefore let us not sleep as others do, but let us watch and be sober' (1 Thessalonians 5:2-6).

Thirdly, do you understand who is dealing with you? If you are late for work, you may have a supervisor who can fire you for not showing up on time. Accountability is what gives punctuality its force. 'It is high time' to wake up spiritually because we are accountable to God, the judge of the living and the dead (1 Peter 4:5).

Catch the vision!

Once we wake up spiritually and 'the eyes of our understanding' are opened (Ephesians 3:1), we need to catch the vision that God has unveiled in his Word — his purpose for our lives.

Firstly, the believer is bound for glory. 'Our salvation is nearer than when we first believed' says our text. Christians have the 'high calling of God in Christ Jesus' (Philippians 3:14). We are closing in on the fulfilment of our eternal hope. This, at any rate, is how we ought to be thinking. It is to our shame that in practice we often treat the hope of heaven as no more than a fallback position. We concentrate on earthly hopes and ambitions — fun and friends, fame and fortune, career advancement and the like. But the word 'salvation' here refers to our final state in glory (Romans 8:18). 'The souls of believers', says The Shorter Catechism, 'are at their death made perfect in holiness, and do immediately pass into glory, and their bodies, still being united to Christ, do rest in their graves till the resurrection.'[2]

Secondly, time is short. 'The night is far spent, the day is at hand' (Romans 13:12). Our heavenly home-going grows as close as the end of our life. The 'day' that is 'at hand', says Robert Haldane, 'is not the day of judgement, but the day of death.'[3] You can, of course, decide to give yourself another ten years to make the decision to follow Christ. But the truth is, that before the day is out you could hear God say: 'This night your soul will be required of you' (Luke

12:20). We have been warned. We have also been called to eternal life. We need to repent towards God and believe in the Lord Jesus Christ. The gospel call is always couched in urgent terms. Call on him today (Hebrews 3:13).

Get with the programme!

What do you do when you wake up? You get washed and dressed; you ponder the day ahead; you prepare for what will hopefully be a fruitful day. In spiritual terms, this is exactly what Paul asks us to do. To get with God's programme — which is, in sum, about moral cleansing, godly conduct and commitment to Christ. First, we should clean up our act. Since it is 'high time to awake', we need to 'put on the armour of light' (Romans 13:12). The 'light' — God's revealed truth — is 'armour' against moral and spiritual darkness. By it, the Holy Spirit furnishes the mind with sanctifying grace. Waking up to the lethal opposition of 'the works of darkness' ought to stimulate us to chart a godly course. Christians are called to 'put on the whole armour of God' and to 'fight the good fight of faith' as 'sons of light and sons of the day' (Ephesians 6:10; 1 Timothy 6:12; 1 Thessalonians 5:5). Second, we must seize the day. Since our salvation is near, we ought to 'walk properly, as in the day' (Romans 13:13). The focus is on our premeditated conduct. What will the Lord find us doing today? If it is to be a day of blessing, then we must fill the day with the obedience of faith. The man who seeks the blessing of God, says the psalmist, 'walks not in the counsel of the ungodly, nor stands in the path of sinners, nor sits in the seat of the scornful' (Psalm 1:1). Rather, 'his delight is in the law of the Lord'. He seizes each day for the Lord.

Third, we should get ready for action. The illustration from clothing is straightforward. Smart people know how to 'dress for success' in daily life. It is all about commitment.

Since the 'night is far spent' and 'the day is at hand' we should 'put on the Lord Jesus Christ' (Romans 13:14). This is the opposite of making 'provision for the flesh, to fulfil its lusts'. Commit to Christ, not to carnality! This contrast carries through every aspect of Christian experience. 'To put on Christ', says John Calvin, 'means our being surrounded and protected in every part by the virtue of His Spirit, and thus rendered fit for the performance of every duty of holiness. For the image of God, which is the only ornament of the soul, is thus renewed in us.'[4] This is what will fit us for heaven. Without Christ, we cannot enter (Matthew 7:21-23). But clothed in Christ, we shall enter into the joy of our Lord (Matthew 25:23).

NOTES

[1] J. Murray, *Collected Writings*, Vol. II (Banner of Truth, 1977) p.166

[2] *Westminster Shorter Catechism* (http://www.reformed.org/documents/WSC_frames.html) Q.37

[3] R. Haldane, *Romans* (Macdonald (nd)) p.590

[4] J. Calvin, *Romans*, Vol. XIX (Baker, 1979) p.490

*There was a certain rich man who was clothed in purple
and fine linen and fared sumptuously every day.
But there was a certain beggar named Lazarus, full of
sores, who was laid at his gate, desiring to be fed with the
crumbs which fell from the rich man's table.
Moreover the dogs came and licked his sores.
So it was that the beggar died, and was carried by the
angels to Abraham's bosom.
The rich man also died and was buried.
And being in torments in Hades, he lifted up his eyes and
saw Abraham afar off, and Lazarus in his bosom. Then he
cried and said, 'Father Abraham, have mercy on me, and
send Lazarus that he may dip the tip of his finger in water
and cool my tongue; for I am tormented in this flame'.
But Abraham said, 'Son, remember that in your lifetime
you received your good things, and likewise Lazarus evil
things; but now he is comforted and you are tormented.
And besides all this, between us and you there is a great
gulf fixed, so that those who want to pass from here to you
cannot, nor can those from there pass to us'.
Then he said, 'I beg you therefore, father, that you would
send him to my father's house, for I have five brothers, that
he may testify to them, lest they also come to this place of
torment'. Abraham said to him, 'They have Moses and the
prophets; let them hear them'. And he said, 'No, Father
Abraham; but if one goes to them from the dead, they will
repent'. But he said to him, 'If they do not hear Moses and
the prophets, neither will they be persuaded
though one rise from the dead'.*

(Luke 16:19-31)

10. ONLY ONE WAY

Jesus told a story about a rich man and a poor man. The two men die. The poor man goes to be with the patriarch Abraham in heaven, but the rich man goes to 'hell'. A conversation follows between the rich man and Abraham, held across 'a great gulf' fixed between them. This was, of course, a parable. It is not a movie of something that actually happened. There are no actual conversations in eternity between the lost and the redeemed. But it does tell us sober truths about what it will mean if we die unforgiven by God.

So now you know why Jesus told such a dark story. He had been teaching quite a few leading truths in that direction: 'You cannot serve God and Mammon' (Luke 16:13); 'Your brother was dead and is alive again' (15:32); 'There is joy in the presence of the angels of God over one sinner who repents' (15:10); 'so likewise, whoever of you does not forsake all that he has, cannot be my disciple' (14:33). It is all about who we will serve and where we will spend eternity! It is about God's provision of a Saviour in the person and work of Jesus Christ. It is about God's love for sinners, whom he seeks out and saves. And it is about our response to his good news about salvation.

Where do you stand?

The story teaches that our circumstances in life are no indication of our standing with God. Inequality is a fact of life in the real world. The rich man is 'filthy rich' and happy. The other man, Lazarus, lives in abject poverty. He has little to be happy about and appears to get no help from

God. The drama of the story is that when they die, there is a great reversal. The rich man is really the poor one, while the poor man is rich in what ultimately matters. What are we to make of it all?

Everybody dies

Better face it now! 'All go to one place' says Solomon, referring to death (Ecclesiastes 3:20). But death is not about vanishing into non-existence, as some think. Life is short but there is life after death. The Bible says: 'it is appointed for men to die once, but after this the judgment' (Hebrews 9:27). We will all give an account to God for the way we spend our lives (Romans 2:6).

Few object to the idea of heaven, but most people prefer to think there is no hell. Yet there is no logic in such a view. If good must be rewarded, then sin must surely be punished. We all face an eternal reckoning.

Riches do not condemn

We need to understand the meaning of Jesus' parable. It does not teach that our eternal future is determined by whether we are rich or poor in this life. The Bible is quite clear that there is nothing wrong in being rich. Wealth can be received and used as a blessing from God (Psalm 112:3). The question is how we use our wealth (whether small or great). What did the rich man do with his riches? He indulged himself and did not lift a finger to help the poor man. Even though Lazarus sat at his very gate, the poor man had to beg even the crumbs from his table.

Why does God give wealth? Answer: 'that [we] may

have something to give him who has need' (Ephesians 4:28). Lazarus, then, was the test that exposed the rich man's heart for what it was — self-centred, self-absorbed, and hardened. He lived for himself. It is no accident that the only person who complains in the parable is the rich man.

Poverty does not save

God is 'full of compassion and gracious ... abundant in mercy' (Psalm 86:15). He chooses 'the weak things of the world to put to shame the things that are mighty' (1 Corinthians 1:27). The gospel is preached particularly 'to the poor'(Luke 4:18). But poverty afflicts good and bad alike: 'As it is with the good man, so it is with the sinner' (Ecclesiastes 9:2). We know from other Scriptures that Lazarus was saved and went to  heaven, not because he was poor, but because God was gracious to him and gave him faith (Ephesians 2:8).

God cares

Lazarus, we read, 'was carried by the angels to Abraham's bosom'. This highlights the fact that the poor man was a true 'child of Abraham'. Like Abraham, he loved and believed God (Galatians 3:6-9). For the Jews, 'Abraham's bosom' was the figurative (not literal) destination of the redeemed. It speaks of God's covenant to save his people from their sins.

This he did through the ultimate 'Seed' of Abraham, Jesus Christ, who died in the sinner's place (Galatians 3:16).

The rich man, being a Jew, regarded himself as a child of Abraham: 'Father Abraham' he cries. But it is not enough to be physically descended from Abraham; to be saved we must share Abraham's faith in God. Whatever his pedigree, the rich man was lost because he loved neither God nor man, but only himself. It is our inward, heart relationship to God that matters, not our outward circumstances. This is Jesus' great point.

There is only one way to heaven, to reconciliation and eternal fellowship with God. That way is Jesus himself — the one Mediator between God and man (1 Timothy 2:5).

No second chance

In the second part of the story, the scene shifts from time to eternity. Jesus relates a conversation between the rich man and Abraham. The rich man's tormented soul utters three appeals.

Firstly, he seeks relief. He asks that Lazarus be sent to cool his tongue with water. Was he repentant for behaviour towards Lazarus? Not for a moment! In hell he remains self-centred, expecting Lazarus to wait upon his needs. In reply, Abraham points out that there is no second chance in eternity. There is 'a great gulf fixed' between heaven and hell. There can be no repentance in eternity; it is unnecessary for the saved and impossible for the lost.

Five brothers

If he can't have the poor man to bring relief for his thirst, the rich man wants something else. Lazarus must become his message-boy to warn his five brothers and save them from a similar fate. He still treats Lazarus as a beggar. There is no sorrow for past behaviour. Even his concern for his brothers may have been self-serving. Having encouraged them on their path to hell, did he now want to be free of the consequences?

Abraham's answer is brief and to the point. But it shows us that God's Word is sufficient for every sinner's need. 'They have Moses and the prophets [the Holy Scriptures]; let them hear them'. How may we be forgiven our sins and fitted for heaven? Jesus answers: 'not by bread alone, but by every word of God' (Luke 4:4). Scripture is the mind of God revealed. It is 'able to make you wise for salvation through faith ... in Christ Jesus' (2 Timothy 3:15). The Bible tells us the way of salvation in Christ.

Are you listening to God?

Repentance

No, says the rich man, God's words will not be enough! It will take a visible miracle to change my brothers' attitudes. So please send Lazarus back as a preacher! If someone rises from the dead they will believe and repent. Signs and wonders seem much more powerful than mere words, even God's words. Abraham's answer is sobering: if people won't listen to God's Word, even raising the dead won't convince them!

And it won't. And for a lot of people it hasn't! Jesus tells us himself that he has given the world exactly one sign — the 'sign of Jonah' (Matthew 12:39-41). He was referring to his own death and resurrection, his victory over death and the grave. The evidence supporting his physical resurrection is compelling. Anyone who has examined the matter will admit this. More than one sceptical writer has set out to disprove the resurrection of Christ, only to be convinced that it really did happen. But few turn from their sin and seek forgiveness as a result.

Only one way

But some do. Some believe and are saved. And where does their faith in Christ come from? 'Faith comes by hearing, and hearing by the word of God', replies the Bible (Romans 10:17). The resurrection of Jesus confirms the truth of the Word of God concerning him. But it is the all-sufficient Word that God, by his Holy Spirit, uses to bring lost people from spiritual darkness to light. God's Word is sufficient and powerful because it is 'sharper than any two-edged sword ... a discerner of the thoughts and intents of the heart' (Hebrews 4:12). It is that Word that tells us that Jesus Christ is the only way of salvation.

'Salvation is found in no one else, for there is no other name under heaven given to men by which we must be saved' (Acts 4:12). What is your hope? Where is your salvation? Who is your Saviour? The rich man was not only a lost sinner in need of a Saviour – he was a lost sinner, in hell forever, who did not want a Saviour. He had made his covenant with death — he was in agreement with hell, had made lies his refuge and hidden himself from God under a covering of falsehoods (Isaiah 28:15). We all stand before the door of eternity. The gospel calls us to new life in the risen Saviour, Jesus Christ. And he assures us that he will not refuse anyone who will believe upon him as the One who is able to save them to the uttermost; 'All that the Father gives me will come to me, and the one who comes to me I will by no means cast out' (John 6:37).